LAST MINUTE MINUTE ROOMS IN BETHLEHEM

AND OTHER GREAT INTERNET SEARCH HISTORIES OF THE PAST

Also by Dale Shaw

Letters of Not
F*ck this Journal

LAST
MINUTE
ROOMS IN
BETHLEHEM

AND OTHER
GREAT INTERNET
SEARCH HISTORIES
OF THE PAST

DALE SHAW

BⵊXTREE

First published 2017 by Boxtree
an imprint of Pan Macmillan
20 New Wharf Road, London N1 9RR
Associated companies throughout the world
www.panmacmillan.com

ISBN 978-0-7522-6629-9

1 3 5 7 9 8 6 4 2

A CIP catalogue record for this book is available from the British Library.

Illustrations © Gwen Burns 2017
Typeset by seagulls.net

Printed and bound by CPI Group (UK) Ltd, Croydon, CR0 4YY

Visit **www.panmacmillan.com** to read more about all our books
and to buy them. You will also find features, author interviews and
news of any author events, and you can sign up for e-newsletters
so that you're always first to hear about our new releases.

For Daisy B.

GOD

Feeling unfulfilled
Do I need a project?
Ship in a bottle?
Those shelves that need putting up?
Creating a universe?
Creating a universe on a budget
Best size for a bang?
Huge bang?
Titchy bang?
Middling bang?
Bang that starts out fairly small and then gets really
    really big?
Universe creation + next steps
Things you typically find in a universe
Appropriate number of stars
How do you get things to stay still and not float off
    everywhere?
Credible planet shapes
Why exactly can't planets be triangles?
Who is making these rules?
Should I stick rings on one?
Sod it, I'm sticking rings on one
Things to stick on planets
Things to stick on planets that squeak
Appropriate names for animals that eat ants
What exactly has hooves?
What exactly are hooves?
Hooven or hooved?
Or Hoover?
Best insect to vomit out honey?

Best number of legs for spiders?
Best number of eyes for spiders?
Same number of eyes as legs + potential issues
Should I give spiders butt ropes for some reason?
Should I be spending less time on spiders?
Will creating mankind come back to haunt me?
Man + nipples + LOLZ
Best pets to keep in a garden
Best talking pets to keep in a garden
Should I store all knowledge of good and evil in some
    sort of fruit?
How big should dinosaurs be?
Keeping millions of dead cavemen entertained
Believing in yourself
Being in two places at once + basic conjuring techniques
Should I throw a wrap party + big bang?
Should I use the 'went with a bang' line at the wrap party?
Winning a crowd back after a poor joke decision
How to know if you're ready to have children

ADAM

Gardening
Gardening while lonely
Passing time in a garden by yourself
Spot the tree + rules
Twig solitaire?
Rib counting
Why do I have a belly button?
Best way to ask your boss for things
Can you live without a rib?
Holy crap, where did she come from?
What do women want?
Best woodland creature to have a discrete affair with
Squirrel seduction techniques
Squirrel dumping techniques
Wife spending too much time with a talking snake + advice
This season's fig leaves
Fig leaves + autumn?
Rebutting accusations of fig-leaf padding
What is sin?
Where is sin?
How much is sin?
What's with all the rhetorical questions?
Things to do when you're not in a garden
Appeals process + God
Negotiating resettlement packages
Why do none of my kids look like me?

EVE

Passing time in a pre-created state
I Spy + something beginning with nothingness
Very difficult hide and seek
Spot the void
When will I ever meet a man?
Is this missing rib significant?
Meeting that special man
What do men want?
Is my partner cheating on me?
Is my partner cheating on me with a woodland creature?
Why do I keep finding acorns in the bedroom?
Why does Adam have nipples?
Apple dos and don'ts
What's the difference between that apple that Adam has
    and an Adam's apple?
Why am I taking relationship advice from a talking snake?
What would happen if I ate the melon that a lizard
    mentioned?
Are grapes recommended by owls OK?
Signs you're allergic to fig leaves
Overcoming mansplaining
Overcoming godsplaining
Why does Adam spend so much time with his friend Steve?
Why did I get the blame for everything + damning all
    humanity
Is childbirth as fun as God says it is?
Can two members of the same sex inbreed?
Local family therapy centres

PALEOLITHIC MAN

Mud
Fire
Mud
Fire
Mud fire
Why no fire from mud?
Why no mud from fire?
Rub mud hard + fire?
Rub mud harder + fire?
Why hand go hurt?
Why Grug have fire?
How get Grug fire?
Stealing fire
Treating burns
Do lady caveman find scars sexy?
What me eat?
Eat mud?
Mud pie?
Rock cakes?
Mud + side dishes
Health benefits of all mud diet
Where all dinosaurs go?
Where Adam and Eve go?
Why Grug only draw bison?
Why Sabre Tooth Tiger always mad at me?
Hitting over head with club + better way to meet women
Is fur murder?
Does 'ug' mean what I think it means?
Cave decoration tips
Are craggy outcrops in this season?

Is it hunt then gather or other way round?
How long this ice age last?
Is puberty also old age?
Why Grug have wheel?
How get wheel?
Stealing wheel
Did I invent getting run over?
Why homo sapiens always so smug?
Where sun go at night?
Where wife go at night?
Why me talk like this + symptoms of stroke

HU BEAKER, STONEHENGE PROJECT MANAGER

Henge
What is a henge?
Don't we mean hinge?
A stone hinge would make a lot more sense
Why is the word henge only applied to this thing?
Am I being pranked?
Getting estimates for henges
WIs pict labour cheap?
Best stone for a henge
Why are the best stones so incredibly far away?
Why can't we use the big rocks that are sitting right there?
Why do all of our many gods love big slabs?
Can you make henges out of other things?
Feather Henge?
Fluff Henge?
Twig Henge?
Shingle henge?
Distance from Wiltshire to Wales

Motivating workers

Motivating flattened workers

What do builders mean when they say they've gone to
   another job?

Surely there must be an easier way to tell the time?

Why are we doing this again?

Getting gravel stains out of hooded cowls

Sacrificing animals + non-icky

Seriously, why are we doing this again?

Hiring local celebrities for opening ceremonies

Famous wizard?

The crone that looks like a turnip?

That man who lived to be an unbelievable 38 years old?

Do we need some sort of gift hut?

What is a solstice anyway?

When do the clocks go back?

Why do we have to get up so bloody early?

Should henges have massive gaps?

Moving henges a few inches to the left

Rental yield on henges

Rental yield on henges + moderate roof issues

NOAH

Climate change
Is climate change real?
Climate change + proof
Climate change + not too much proof
Pretty crazy shiz + messages from God
Should I always listen to God?
How to build a boat
How to build a big bastard boat
How to build a big bastard boat in a hurry
How to build a big bastard boat in a hurry THAT'S
    ALSO A ZOO
Can't God just magic me up a boat?
Having a boss that makes unreasonable demands
What exactly is an ark?
Why is it called an ark?
Is ark just a fancy word for a boat?
I don't really have time for fancy words when I'm
    currently gathering every animal IN THE WORLD
Delegating tasks
Delegating tasks + high probability of mauling
Basic herding techniques
Sexing mosquitoes
Overcoming allergies
Do any animals actually like each other?
How to temporarily stop animals from mating
Chastity belts + every animal ever + delivery
Are fish on the list?
If so, why?
And insects? Why include insects?
Birds too? WHAT IS THIS CRAP?

Shouldn't I be helping
   people before squirrels?
Do we just float in one place
   or are we supposed to go
   somewhere?
Is this a test?
Is God a dick?
Is that God I hear laughing?
Kicking penguins into submission
Appropriate monkey punishments
Things to poke bears with
Will I smell like dung forever?
Can I just drop off all the animals in the same place?
Staying on dry land for the rest of your life
Really extravagant gifts for wives

OEDIPUS

Laughing off prophecies

Getting money back + Delphi

How to meet very familiar looking women in the
Thebes area

Bagging a total MILF

Is there any reason I should pay more attention to my
romantic conquests?

Coping with unsettling news

Counselling

Really good counselling

Probably not family counselling

Erasing mental images

How long should I wait to call after a date + own
mother?

Catchy things to say immediately after sleeping with
your own mother

'That takes me back'

'I'm one bad motherfunker'

'Now that's what I call a mummy issue!'

Suitable mothers day gifts + you know what

Am I now my own uncle?

Appropriate jokes + family get-togethers

Should I brag to my mates about this?

Innovative second date ideas + own mother

Would granny like to get in on this?

Making small talk + pretty bad incest

Things I have in common with my dad

Explaining things to dad

What happened to dad?

Chances of getting a son of the year award

Should I appear in the amphitheatre alongside Jerimius
    Kyleanthe?
Wiping the smug expression off the face of an oracle
Isn't this a bit messed up even for ancient Greece?
Ensuring the story of your life doesn't fall into the
    'comedy' category
Ocular ways of making amends
Upsides of sudden self-inflicted blindness
Blindness + better hearing?
Blindness + free dog?
Not being able to see the expressions on other family
    members faces?
Did I give love a bad name?
What am I the king of?
Am I the king of being a really crappy son?
Ensuring your legacy is not all about the incest
Getting your name removed from complexes

ODYSSEUS

Where is Troy?
Is Paris in Troy?
Why is our geography so confusing?
Am I Ulysses as well?
Should I be getting two pay cheques?
Things to occupy wives during potentially long work trips
Things to launch ships with other than beautiful
   women's faces
Oh crap, did I forget my keys?
On a scale from one to ten how gullible are Trojans?
Weird ways to win sieges
Very quiet lumberjacking
What's the best large wooden animal to hide inside?
Large Wooden Duck?
Large Wooden Duck-Billed Platypus?
Large Wooden Sprat?
Large Wooden Badger?
Large Wooden Ant?
Large Wooden Hyena?
Large Wooden Gibbon?
Large Wooden Guppy?
Large Wooden Weasel?
Large Wooden Sea Lion?
Large Wooden Woodlouse?
Large Wooden Giant Squid?
Large Wooden Vampire Bat?
Large Wooden Amoeba?
Suppressing sniggering inside large wooden horses
Good things to shout when leaping from a large
   wooden horse

'Don't mean to nag, but you got Greeked!'

'Why the long face?'

'Troy this on for size!'

How not to look too smug when slaughtering enemies

Directions: Troy to Greece

Directions: Troy to Greece + scenic route

Fancy names for long journeys

Why is it called an odyssey?

Oh wait, is it called an odyssey because I'm Odysseus?
    I just got that!

After that war, the journey home will be a piece of
    cake, right?

What's with all the freaky creatures that weren't there
    when we were travelling in the other direction?

Good gifts for spouses when you've been away for ages

PLATO

Professions for people who don't like heavy lifting
Professions for people who don't really like doing anything
Is there a way to get paid for sort of staring off into the
    distance?
Things philosophers tend to say
How exactly do I make money from this?
Should I go door to door and ask people if they want any
    philosophizing done?
Having a trade to fall back on
Restauranteur? My name does have plate in it
Do I have superpowers which allow me to take on the
    characteristics of a plate? If so, how would that be
    helpful?
Does having one name make
    you cooler?
Good surnames if your
    first name is Plato
Beans?
My Giddy Aunt?
Pen Sesame?

LET ME GUESS,
IT'S A PLATE

Good word for talking about the thinginess of things

Socrates

Isn't Socrates great?

Extolling the virtues of Socrates

Best way to tell Socrates that he's your best friend

Socrates + news

Socrates + arrest + corrupting youth?

Socrates + execution?

Not really being that much into Socrates after all

Distancing yourself from that whole Socratic area

Meeting girls

It's ancient Greece, why can't I get any action?

Why do girls keep telling me they like me 'as a friend'?

What is a 'friend zone'?

Do they need philosophers in Kavos?

Do they need erotic philosophers in Kavos?

Do I overthink things?

How many times can I get away with the 'it's all greek to
    me' joke?

Why aren't there any clean-shaven philosophers?

Starting a school

Stuff you need to start a school

Job lot of blackboards

Loads of chairs

Basic grasp of Greek

Good names for schools

'Plato's Super Special Academy for Clever Cloggers'?

'The Study Zone and Soft Play Area'?

'Professor Brainbox's Infotainemal Funzerversity'?

Subtle ways to tell Aristotle he's a bit of a smart arse

Is metaphysics just physics that constantly mentions itself
    in an annoying way?

ALEXANDER THE GREAT

Surnames
Aspirational surnames
Really aspirational surnames
Alexander the Nifty?
Alexander the Truly Superb?
Alexander the Pretty Dang Sweet?
Does 'Al the Great' sound less showy-offy?
How about Alexander the Great Looking (am I right?)
What does over-compensation mean?
Having dads murdered + benefits
Why is my mum such a total pain about me
    murdering my dad?
Stifling laughter + parental funeral oration
Benefits of thinking you're completely
    indestructible
Am I a god or just really really
    handsome?
Why is winning battles so easy?
Damn, how do I look so stunning
    in a toga?
Basic knot untying
Basic knot untying + shortcuts
Going rate + women and children
Coming up with names for vanquished cities
Coming up with names for vanquished cities
    that don't have Alexander in the name
Coming up with names for vanquished cities
    that have multiple Alexanders in the name
How to keep cartographers on their toes

Tempering self-doubt via large-scale land grabs

How can I be so good at conquering and so rubbish at conkers?

How to cope with basically perfect hair

Upkeep of washboard abs

Pitfalls of flawless skin

Looking less spectacular on a big horse

Papering over glaring personality flaws + big horse

Is my middle name 'the'?

How come everyone acts so busy when I walk into the room?

How am I allowed to get away with all this stuff?

How can I look so fine even with an arrow sticking out of me?

Ways to avoid library fines + fire

Things to do before Jesus turns up

Nice places to visit + India

Empire building for dummies

What to do when there are no more lands to conquer + charades?

Why didn't daddy hug me more?

Am I so great?

PYTHAGORAS

What's my angle?
Am I too obtuse?
Is arithmetic the same as maths?
Good ways to cheat at maths
Writing sums on my toga flaps?
Abacus under beard?
Fractions on inside of eyelids?
Why can't I master my seven times table?
Why aren't girls impressed by my remarkable
    mathematical skills?
Can I come up with a theory to help me meet cute girls
    in my area?
Why do I always have to divide the bill after big meals?
How can nothing plus nothing be nothing + witchcraft?

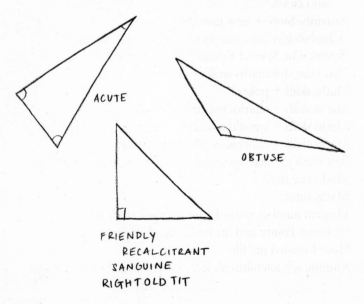

ACUTE

OBTUSE

FRIENDLY
   RECALCITRANT
    SANGUINE
RIGHT OLD TIT

How big is a hypotenuse?

Do hypotenuses bite?

Am I strange for checking under my bed for hypotenuses every night?

What's the difference between a theory and a theorem?

Should I shout 'ta-da!' after explaining my whole triangle thing?

How to make tons of money from the corners of triangles

Cracking shapes other than triangles

Is there cash in parallelograms?

Trying to come up with slightly more exciting theories

Explaining why my particular skills don't help in assembling furniture

Boat parties with students

Covering up non-accidental student drownings

Would inventing some new numbers make me look big and clever?

'Shivinty-Stoo' + new number?

'Chadwick' + new number?

'Seven: The Special Edition' + new number?

Can I use this maths stuff at the racetrack?

Maths skills + poker?

Maths skills + chariot racing?

Maths skills + wrestling odds?

Maths skills + enormous gambling debts?

Best ways to make some quick money from my skills

Maths teacher?

Maths tutor?

Magical number wizard who appears at kid's parties?

Professor Pointy and his funky number-puppets?

Have I wasted my life?

Ruining schoolchildren's lives for years and years to come

HANNIBAL

Battle techniques
Surprising enemies
Surprising enemies + incongruous animals
Crossing mountains on many ducks?
Crossing mountains on a legion of hedgehogs?
Crossing mountains on a phalanx of newts?
Crossing mountains on a retinue of koalas?
Number of hummingbirds to lift one soldier?
Wait a minute, what about horses?
What's like a horse but greyer, needlessly huge and
    infinitely harder to source?
Selling ideas to sceptical troops + elephants
Is a pachyderm the same as an elephant?
Are elephants cheaper to buy or rent?
Do elephants like snow?
Can elephants eat snow?
Selling elephant dung + alps area
Oversized trunk warmers + bulk buy
When is it my turn on the elephant?
Good names for elephants
'Hannibal Jr'?
'Trunky'?
'Sir Plops a Lot'?
Getting those animal rights people off your back
Re-establishing your legacy
Trying to move away from that whole elephant thing
Pointing out to people that there weren't *that* many
    elephants
Highlighting strategic abilities over elephant use
How to make people forget all about the elephants

Forming a rag-tag team to distract from elephant
    exploitation

What do I need to form a good team?

Should I recruit Murdockus Murdimus despite his
    reported insanity?

Would Antilles Phace be a useful member of the team?

How about the warrior known only as T?

Is T too aggressive and bejewelled to be a successful
    team member?

Why won't T get on top of an elephant?

Ways to subdue T so he gets onto an elephant

Why is T always pitying fools?

Elation connected to a plan coming together

JULIUS CAESAR

Avoiding vaginas during birth
Salads
Innovative salads
Is salad my only friend?
Pushing your salad agenda via world domination
Getting salads named after you
Roman vs romaine
Cucumber + hmmmmm?
Why hot food is an affront to nature
Soup + world's greatest malfeasance
Grilling + vile
Good names for my salad fanzine
'Lettuce Pray'?
'Dressing for Dinner'?
'Cold Leafy Facts'?
'Salad Daze'?
Could I make a crouton my consul?
What salads do they have in Gaul?
Why fruit salad is an abomination
Fruit salad consumption + instant crucifixion
Exciting creamy dressings
Good rivers to cross to prove a point
Why are roman numerals so hard?
What should I do after coming and seeing?
Could aqueducts help speed up salad preparation?
What salads do they have in Britain?
Leaving Britain as quickly as possible + no salad +
    all chips
What salads do they have in Egypt?
What to do if your girlfriend doesn't like your salad?

How to get eye make-up out of robes
Getting sand out of coleslaw
First act as dictator + outlawing stews?
Why do our calendars go backwards?
Trying to sound sexy + Latin
Trying to sound sexy + salads
Wait, can I put laurel leaves in a salad + excitement!!!
Carrots yay or nay?
Am I allergic to ass's milk?
Ass's milk + hygiene + euphemism
Bros before Egyptian hoes
What is an ide?
Should I be worried about ides?
Why has Brutus circled the ides on my stupid backwards
    calendar?
How best friends are great and never betray you
Memorable last words
Memorable last salads
Staunching many stab wounds with lettuce

CLEOPATRA

Buying eyeliner in bulk

Innovative fringe motifs

Am I just Queen of the Nile or some other rivers as well?

Marrying own brother + non-awkward seating plans

Making an entrance via floor coverings

Killing time in a carpet

Treating rug burns

Wouldn't lino make for an easier exit?

Casual ways to buy poison in bulk

Witty things to say to Italians

Italian men + drawbacks + tiny leather skirts

Do I have a fetish + Italians

Simple pasta dishes to impress your man

Can I just dress up as myself for Halloween?

Good places to commit infidelity in a pyramid

Does all this chunky golden jewellery really suit me?

What to do with a load of old milk

How to make yoghurt

Can you even milk an ass?

Unrealistic lactose demands

Why is there no word for a lady pharaoh?

'Pharette'?

'Heraoh'?

'King Tit'?

Latin for headache

Is there any better air conditioning than wafted palm
   fronds?

Why are ancient Egyptians on walls always pointing in
   that one direction?

This season's overly ornate sandals

How many poisonings is just too many poisonings?
Why does Caesar like hail so much?
Dumping emperors obsessed with salad
Meeting emperors' friends who aren't obsessed with salad
Do I call him Mark or Antony?
Why the phrase 'you can't take it with you' shouldn't
    apply to me
Uses for a soiled toga
What's our deal with cats?
Ostentatious barge wholesalers
Wacky suicide attempts + reptiles
Will I be a yummy mummy?

VIRGIN MARY

Breaking news
Breaking surprising news
Breaking really surprising news
Breaking news + delicately
Breaking news + delicately + husband
Breaking news + delicately + husband + angel +
    knocked up
Effective cleaning methods + broken furniture
Effective cleaning methods + homemade broken furniture
Pregnancy
Reasons for pregnancy
Reasons for pregnancy + weird
Reasons for pregnancy + weird + God
Conflict resolution
Conflict resolution + husband
Conflict resolution + husband + God
Summoning angels
Summoning convincing angels
Angel costumes + cheap + Nazareth
Last minute rooms in Bethlehem
Why is it always so busy over Christmas?
Traveling while pregnant
Pregnant + donkey + disease?
Pregnant + stable + disease?
Dangers of hay fever + childbirth
Entertaining shepherds at short notice
Squeezing things out of your vagina with shepherds
    watching
Hebrew for 'push'
These guys don't seem that wise + vague star navigation

Why is that kid with the drum in here?
Kosher placenta recipes
Should I breastfeed + Son of God
Interesting baby names
'Fesus'?
'Jebus'?
'Greasehouse'?
How can you turn a halo off?
Disposing of unwanted gifts + Myrrh
What is swaddling?
Should I swaddle?
Did I just swaddled?
Should I ask you-know-who for child support?

JESUS

What does the H stand for?

Faking it + carpentry

Good names for father and son carpentry companies

'We've Got Wood'

'Working Miracles in Mahogany'

'Get Thee Behind Me, Bargains!'

Good gifts for Mother's Day + tea towel again?

How to get your centre parting extra sharp

Will anyone ever write a song about me?

Ideal amount of time to spend in the wilderness

Is the wilderness nice?

Wilderness + fun things to do

Good symbols for gangs

Good names for gangs

'The Bethlehem Bunch'?

'Sandy and the Fish Separators'?

'The Gallillegion of Honour'?

Am I Mexican?

Would my skills be better served in catering?

How come all my money gets split three ways?

Best flowers to consider

Roses of the mountain?

Daffodils of the gorge?

Buddlia of the swamp?

Why is Paul constantly taking notes?

Open-toe inflatable aqua sandals + patent

Local raised areas that are ideal for making a sermon on

Stopping apostles making that booing sound every time
     Mary Magdalene walks in

Improving on the line 'take up thy bed and walk'

'Grab your duvet and sashay!'
'Get outta here, you big lug'
'Now that's what I call a mattress topper!'
Where to get a 'lepers by appointment only' sign made
Places to borrow money + Judea
Last-minute dinner locations + table for 13 + Mt Zion
Can we all sit on one side of the table?
Why is Judas always doing that shifty eye thing?
Delicately stopping your mother from attending all your
    performances
Great crucifixion one-liners
'Nailed it!'
'Boy, am I cross'
'Wow, what's the Latin for "subtle"?'
Things to do in a cave for 3 days
Should I leave a note?
Staging dramatic comebacks

BOUDICA

How do you pronounce my name?
Why do people keep trying to sell me pink weaponry?
Should you apply woad on public transport?
Obvious Roman weak points
Roman nose?
Roman temple?
Up the Appian Way?
Colchester hotspots
Getting men to stop explaining how to use an axe
How do you spell my name?
This season's Celtic brooches
Looking good in a helmet and no top
Effective names for military operations
'Operation Impending Victory'?
'Operation Resplendent Eagle'?
'Operation Pull Those Roman Lungs Out'?

Do I possibly hold grudges for too long?

Latin for 'Jive Turkey'

Basics of enemy impalement

Do they hate me because I'm a woman?

Do they hate me because I'm ginger?

Do they hate me because I keep stabbing them
with things?

Attaching those spike things to cartwheels

What's so great about aqueducts anyway?

Straight roads + overrated

Olive oil + nowhere near as good as lard

How to produce a blood curdling scream and still
be ladylike

Making it clear you're not just doing this 'for attention'

Taking your kids to work day

Do I have a last name?

Good titles to adopt once I've won this thing

'Queen Boudica of all the Britons (Who Aren't Dead)'?

'Empress Boudica of Everywhere Including Here'?

'Goddess Boudica (The Humble)'?

What do you call the Romans who are from other bits
of Italy?

ATTILA THE HUN

Good one-liners to shout when vanquishing enemies
'You've been hunned!'
'You just joined the Attila flotilla (of dead people)'
'You're a goth, you should enjoy being in pain'
'Red's your colour'
'At least you'll save money on haircuts'
'Tell your god, he's next'
'Time to get attilannihilated'
'Fancy some béarnaise sauce with your stake (through
    the throat)'
'Your dark ages just got darker'
'Hey Roman, you're done roamin''
'Look at the mess you made, messy'
'You OK hun?'
'It must be love because you just got an arrow through
    the heart'
'It must be love because you just got a great big cleaver
    through the forehead'
'I hate to Vandalize, but . . .'
'Nice to see you've got guts'
'You used to have a good head on your shoulders'
'I'm a nomad. You're a no nads'
'You got sacked, Jack'
'I admire your Latin tongue. Shame it's all the way
    over there'
'You're not a lot of Gaul (any more)'
'Are you a buttload of horses? Because I just owned
    you, bitch'
'This is gonna look great in a renaissance-era masterpiece'
'I had a brother called Bleda. You're a lot like him'

'Holy Roman Empire? Well, now you're the holy part
(because you have holes in you)'
'Hunny, I'm home!'
'Great, now I have to add sword cleaning to my chore list'
'I see your blood type is . . . everywhere'
'You've got a nerve. I can see one dangling right there'
'You look taller lying down'
'Let me have a stab at it. Oh, I just did'
'I feel like I know you inside out'
'Nice John the Baptist impression'
'Is your first name Pierce?'

KING ARTHUR

Issues

Issues + really weird childhood

Did a wizard really raise me or is that just a repressed
    memory?

Is the sword in the stone or do I get stoned with a sword?

Do I need to get a big fork to go with the big knife?

Methods for sterilizing giant cutlery

Good names for swords

'Stabsworth'?

'Sir Pokeington'?

'The Excallibrator'?

Should I trust a lady in a lake?

Are women in canals any more trustworthy?

Chicks in lagoons + trustworthiness

Females in puddles + honesty

Life decisions + chick in a watery inlet

General advice from the very damp

Freshwater dwelling female + potential STDs

Genital fin rot?

Will she be really pruny?

Will she constantly have swimmers' ear?

Am I being catfished?

Reservoir lady

Reservoir lady + good name for a song?

Should I start a soft rock band?

Kickass lute players + Avalon area

If Avalon is an island why is she in a lake?

Accepting swords from wet women

Wait, is this the same sword as before or a different sword?

Why do I keep getting free swords from people?

KNIGHTS OF THE BRAVE DEEDS
KNIGHTS OF THE FAMED BRAVERY
KNIGHTS OF DERRING-DO
KNIGHTS WHO ARE THE SLAYERS OF EVIL
KNIGHTS OF SELFLESS HEROISM

WHAT SHAPE SHOULD THE TABLE BE?

Shape options for knight tables
Levelling the status of knights via a round table
The man wearing the crown is clearly still in charge, right?
Why is Lancelot so great?
Perfect gifts for Lancelots?
Is Lancelot my BFF?
Looking for Lancelot
Lancelot sightings + Camelot area
Lancelot + queen + rumours
Why are people called Lancelot such cheating arseholes?
Meeting women + Shalott area
Avoiding women + Shalott area

ERIC BLOODAXE, VIKING

Why are our boats so long?
What should be the rough ratio of pillaging to raping?
Non-fruity beard plaits
Best kindling + Viking funerals
Is burning ships really that cost effective?
Who is Val Halla?
Should I lend money to Eric Baddebt?
Getting blood out of broadswords
Getting blood out of double-headed axes
Getting blood out of leather tunics
Getting blood out of pretty much everything
Hygge basics
Non-dreary rowing dirges
Advantages to a horned helmet
Should I have Eric Toiletclogger as a houseguest?
Why are our houses so long?
Good things to bellow at monks
Why is burning stuff so much fun?
Things to do in York
Should we establish our Viking centre in York?
Why can't we invade somewhere warm?
Why getting all greased up and wrestling naked with your
     shipmates is not 'mildly homoerotic'
Will shields get rusty if they're on the outside of the boat?
Why do monks make that noise when you hit them?
Who are you calling Cnut?
How do you ride a Valkyrie?
Should I trust Eric Ericstabber?

Stopping ale from pouring out the eyeholes when drinking
from skulls

Should I get a Celtic tattoo?

Good souvenirs to bring back for wives

Good non-horrific souvenirs to bring back for wives

What's a better navigation method, maps or punching the
sea in the face?

Are there any other books than *Beowulf*?

Should I let my daughter date Eric Punchdaughter?

Should we attack that king called Unready or is it a trap?

Why are our swords so long?

Hats + branding + ideas

Why are monks so annoying?

Why is everything such a saga?

OK, SO NONE OF US KNOW WHAT PILLAGING MEANS...

LADY GODIVA

Bets
Reneging on bets
Reneging on stupid drunken bets
Why do I always get pissed and agree to this sort of thing?
Am I a ladette?
Do I really have to go full commando?
Overcoming chafing
Overcoming equine chafing
Overcoming extreme equine chafing
Growing your hair really long and really quickly
Am I an exhibitionist?
Am I a bit of a perv?
Could I get some sort of grant for this + performance art?
Should I be doing this for charity?
Can you hire full-length flesh-coloured body stockings?
What colour horse will make me look my skinniest?
Ladylike + definition
Statutes on public nudity
Statues of public nudity
What if I get a taste for this sort of thing?
Estimated temperature + Coventry + Saturday
Would it be cheating to keep my vest on?
If nobody's looking, can't I just walk through town fully
      clothed with some coconuts?
What diseases can you catch from a horse's back?
Ways to dissuade your husband from going into Coventry
      town centre on Saturday
How to avoid being slut-shamed
How to suddenly say that something was a sort of protest
Things people protest against

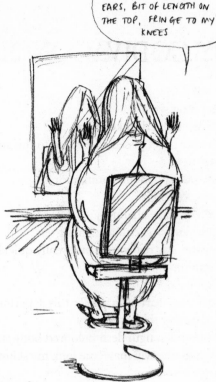

Taxes?

Injustice?

Public indecency?

Preventing the sale of bootleg etchings

Lying to horse rental companies

Getting deposit back + rented horses + emotionally
    scarred

Will this get into the Domesday Book?

Semi-clothed sheep herding in Redditch?

Erotic egg collecting in Stoke?

Tits-out goat milking in Walsall?

How come the peeping bloke is arguably more famous
    than me?

Naked public equestrianism + nobody will remember
    this, right?

WILLIAM THE CONQUERER

Which one of us is Norman?
Hastings + best time to go?
Stifling laughter + regal eye injuries
King names
Good king names
Good non-boastful king names
William the Winner?
William the Frankly Ace?
Billy the Brilliant?
Assimilation + European migrant
The English
English habits
Non-horrifying English habits
How to stop an entire nation smelling of merde
Casually dropping the concept of washing into
    conversations with subjects
Ratio of harridans to damsels + England
Froggy Bellend + meaning?
Winning-over peasants
Defeating peasants
Punishing peasants
Crushing peasants
Anglo Saxon cuisine
Anglo Saxon cuisine + real?
How to impose your culture on others in a nice way
How to impose your culture on others in a violent way
How not to come across as too French
Is beef the same as a cow?
Can someone remind me why I invaded this dump?
Why is all English cheese so bland?

Why is all English wine so non-existent?

How do the English come up with such vile pie fillings on
    such a regular basis?

What is wrong with English mouths?

Winning hearts and minds

Eating hearts and minds

Should I worry about allies invading Normandy?

Are Normans good at anything other than arches?

Bayeux Tapestry corrections

Bayeux Tapestry + William + a bit too fat?

Good names for books

'Happy Book'?

'Everything's OK Book'?

'Nowhere Near Domesday   LE TAPESTRY CUSS
    Book'?

Hiring census takers +
    trustworthy

Dictatorship + not
    trying too hard

Dictating from a distance

Dictating from a distance
    + Normandy

Holidays in the Dordogne

GENGHIS KHAN

What to do with big piles of severed arms
How to appear nonchalant while slaughtering
Effective troop management through gross atrocities
How carby are enemies' hearts?
Quiz + how barbarian am I?
Why do human bodies have all that weird stuff inside?
Would a severed head on top of my own head suit me?
Is wearing someone else's face on your face bad luck?
How to tell if your troops are afraid of you
Effective angry faces
Is it classy to leave one finger unbroken?
Using a spinal cord for a belt
Instilling fear in your foes via all sorts of nastiness
Could showing someone their spleen before they die be
    a thing?
Best beard designs for noted psychopaths
Easy to remember brain recipes
Creative ideas for hideous murder
Practical solutions for discarded shins
Time saving eye-gouge techniques
Good ways to describe that sound pelvises make when
    they come off
Am I mean?
Am I a big meanie?
Where am I going in my life?
Ways to maintain bloodlust
Rekindling the urge to eviscerate
Going through the vanquishing motions
Am I getting enough out of nostril splitting?
More to life + running someone over with lots of horses

WHO CAN BRUTALLY SUBJEGATE YOU?

GENGHIS KHAN

Signs you're getting jaded
Sounds of skulls being crushed + meh
Kneecap extraction + joie de vivre
A sort of general yanking-off-thumbs malaise
Stuck in a rut + disembowelling
Is there more to life than indiscriminate slaughter?
Questioning your entire impaling lifestyle
Talking sensitively to your enemy before their throat fills
   with blood
Do I need career break?
How to stop people making that 'Genghis Can't' joke

ROBIN HOOD

Is merry a euphemism for something?
Dropping casual hints about personal hygiene + friars
Convincing certain Merry Men not to do that thing
    in trees
Convincing certain Merry Men not to do that thing
    with trees
Would stealing from poor and giving to rich be easier?
More traditional investment opportunities in Greater
    Nottingham area
Poor + rate of return?
Serfs + interest rates?
Peasants + financial security?
Buy-to-let hovels
Why are they so poor anyway?

I WOULDN'T SAY WE'RE RICH. I MEAN, WE'RE COMFORTABLE

Are peasants terrible with money?

Is there any point giving peasants more money?

Why are the poor such ungrateful dicks?

Am I a socialist?

Am I an idiot?

Is my understanding of economics flawed at best?

Cutting overheads + being basically homeless

Shouldn't we build a few rudimentary huts or are we
   really that lazy?

Does Richard really have a lion's heart + freak show

Does the king have any other big-cat body parts?

Good excuses for not going on crusades

Jokes about quivers

Non-obvious jokes about quivers

Convincing Merry Men not to do that thing with voles

What does maid mean?

Does maid mean old?

Does maid mean virgin?

Is she going to be Maid Marian for ever?

Good nicknames for tall people

Is sheriff an elected position or just some bloke with
   a badge?

Tight repair + Sherwood area

Male tight repair + Sherwood area

Basic treehouse construction

Basic splinter removal

Have I got lyme disease?

Inserting lutes into troubadours

Will Scarlet? If not, why not?

Why archery is way better than jousting

Convincing Merry Men not to do that thing with bracken

Is green my colour?

THE WIFE OF BATH

Basic story structure
Do I need to make my protagonist more sympathetic?
What is my inciting incident?
Did I hit all my plot beats?
Should I basically shoehorn more shagging in there?
Should I change my main character from a kangaroo
    to a knight?
What exactly is a book?
Ways to pass the time in Canterbury
How to tell a story
How to tell a story + just shouting in a tavern?
Getting pissed and talking to writers + drawbacks?
Geoffrey Chaucer
Geoffrey Chaucer + trustworthy?
Geoffrey Chaucer + chances of portraying me in a
    good light?
Feigning interest when being subjected to stories
    from millers
Do all great works of literature have lots of fart jokes?
Fascinating things pilgrims do
Am I married to the whole of Bath?
Is my husband an actual bath?
Should I try to be the face of all toothless crones?
How bawdy should I be?
Is it better to be bawdy or ribald?
Dispelling gender stereotypes
Dispelling gender stereotypes via fart jokes
Royalty rates
What is a royalty rate?
What is a Medieval royalty rate?

What should I be getting for *Canterbury Tales*?
Is the Pardoner getting more than me?
Do I need a new agent?
Do I need a new jerkin?
Why wasn't I invited to the launch party?
Launch party + was it the fart jokes?
Misrepresentation
Suing for libel

THE PIED PIPER

What exactly makes me pied?
Why am I a piper when I play the flute?
Shouldn't I be called the Non-Pied Flautist?
Is this really the best way to deal with vermin +
    wind instrument
Flute + intriguing + other household pests?
Can I magically enchant moths with my flute music?
Subduing wasps with a recorder
Dispersing unwanted bats with a swanee whistle
Hiding the fact that your flute is stuffed with cheese
Hiding the fact that you're surprised as anyone that this
    whole rat/flute thing worked
What to do with a sudden buttload of rats
How long should I wait for an invoice to be paid?
Revenge on cheapskates
Flaming bag of dog poop on doorstep?
Steal garden ornaments?
Magically enchant then kidnap all their children?
Filling a flute with sweets
Why are children so easily led?
Childcare dos and don'ts
Plans you didn't really think through

Can children eat rats?
Can rats eat children?
Rat/children recipes
Keeping kids entertained
Keeping rats entertained
Keeping kids/rats entertained + flute
Going rate for babysitters + Saxony
Can rats be trained to babysit?
Exploiting sudden large amounts of children
Sweatshop?
Criminal urchin gang?
Children's choir?
Children's choir + flute
Children's choir + flute + cha-ching!
Booking agents in Hamelin area
Good names for bands
'The Juvenile Kidnap Victims'?
'The Overfilled Cave Dwellers'?
'Barry and the Hamelinites'?
Can you train rats to play musical instruments?
Tour essentials + children + flute
Coping with bad reviews
Revenge on critics + flute

JOAN OF ARC

Why does everything suck?
Why does Brigitte suck?
Painting your room black so you can write poetry in it
Why are my parents such dicks?
Should I start calling myself Jojo?
How come Johannes Ockeghem is such a total babe?
Is Johannes Ockeghem single?
Stopping Brigitte from marrying Johannes Ockeghem
Best medieval acne cures
Why don't my parents understand me or my early music?
Voices
Hearing voices
Can you make money from voices in the head?
Am I special?
Am I mental?
Am I a ventriloquist?
Telling people they have gross bad breath
Telling deities they have gross bad breath
Why does God always want to talk to me during my
    'special private time'?
Does God 'like' me, like me?
Is the king hot?
Should I start calling myself J.O.A.?
Banging new vespers
Does this rough hessian cloth I wear as a rudimentary
    garment make me look fat?
Why are we the only local family with 'of' in our name?
If we move towns does my last name change?
Why can't I wear the vestments that I want to wear?
Why are seven-hour Latin masses so BORING?

I MEAN, PART OF ME WANTS TO LEAD THE KING'S ARMIES IN OUR RIGHTEOUS STRUGGLE AGAINST THE ENGLISH HORDES, AND PART OF ME WANTS TO GET A PIERCING, YOU KNOW?

What is this strange monthly stigmata appearing in
my underpants?
Most attractive severe bowl haircuts for teens
Good training bra for medieval battles
Battles are literally THE WORST
Why does everyone else look better in armour than me?
What to do when other generals are being complete
bitches and whispering when you're trying to give an
inspiring speech
Why does Brigitte think she's better than me?
Should I start calling myself The Arcster?
Why is Brigitte such a bitch?
Why do I have such strange feelings and downy
hair growth?

CHRISTOPHER COLUMBUS

What's the ideal profession for someone with no
    discernible sense of direction?
How to make a stupid boat go in a straight line
Disguising overt queasiness
How to tell a cabin boy about your feelings
Good board games for long voyages
How many mermaids will I see?
Can you catch scurvy from kissing a crew member
    with scurvy?
Pranks involving telescopes + revenge
What's the difference between a boat and a ship?
Roughly which way is west?
Pretending you know how to use one of those pointy
    navigational boat things
Driving a boat while wearing great big lacy sleeves
Why isn't the cabin boy returning my calls?
Why doesn't anyone like my poop deck joke?
Why are jellyfish so weird and creepy and scare me?
Apologizing to the first mate + confusing job titles
What do the sails do?
Why is he called a cabin boy when he refuses to enter
    my cabin?
Why is every single member of the crew in the crow's nest
    + am I a good boss?
Shapes the world usually is
Should I send someone ahead in a dinghy to make sure we
    don't go over the horizon?
Styling out enormous navigational errors

Why spices are overrated anyway
Getting newly discovered lands named after you
Good names for recently discovered lands
'New Better Portugal'?
'The United States of This Guy Right Here!'?
'Columbica'?
'Land of Conveniently Ignoring the People Who Were
    Already Here'?
'New World' + maybe a bit too much?
Promising to name it after the cabin boy if he's extra nice
    to me
Blankets as currency + ahead of my time?
What does indigenous mean?
Calling people Indians who aren't from India +
    politically correct?
Getting those guys to teach me that rain dance thing
Transatlantic slavery + potential historical repercussions
Why didn't I find any potatoes?
Turning the cabin boy into a cabin man

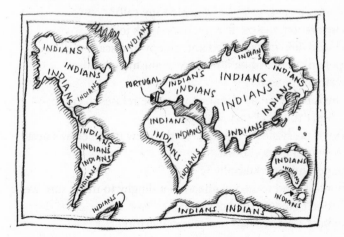

LEONARDO DA VINCI

Bullying
Overcoming bullying
Overcoming renaissance bullying
Why does Pietro hate me?
Being bullied for superior intelligence
Getting bullied for using phrases like 'super intelligence'
Who smeared my easel with dog dirt?
Machines
Machines for revenge
Machines + revenge + bullies + rotor blades
Why 'Professor Thinksalot' is such a hurtful name
Why painting isn't wussy
Art + manliness
How to stop Pietro calling you 'Re-Gaysance Man'
How not to cry when the big boys throw figs at you
How did Pietro legally change my name to Leonardo
    Da Wimpy?
How can I recreate the colour of my purple nurple?
Why my big floppy artist hat isn't 'lame'
Asking Michelangelo to help with bullies
Stopping Michelangelo from joining in with bullies
How can someone have a 'girl's beard'?
Defeating bullies through logic
Defeating bullies through maths
Defeating bullies through engineering
Defeating bullies through running away to France
Overly heterosexual smocks
Why are the massively intellectual so victimised?
Why do I ask questions like that + beaten up
Developing deltoids

What is a deltoid?
Studying anatomy to find out what a deltoid is
Can popes bully you?
Being bullied by popes
Retrieving notebooks from local thugs
Erasing slurs from notebooks
How do bullies always know when I'm going to the toilet?
Removing moustaches from portraits + Mona Lisa
Inventing something to stop my constant sobbing
How to leave messages for big dumb bullies in the future
    via some sort of stupid code

MONA LISA

Resting bitch face + definition

MACHIAVELLI

Am I too nice?
Charity work + Florence area
How to do good things anonymously
Is it possible to over-tithe?
How to help orphans
How to help kittens
How to help orphaned kittens
Gorgeous things to do for people
Allowing local homeless to sleep in your bed
Basic first aid + injured woodland creatures
Giving strangers the shirt off your back + literally
Teaching autistic ducklings to swim
Cleaning up dog poop by my own volition
Leaving flowers for grieving war widows
Turning down numerous civic honours
Telling random pedestrians how much you like their hat
Passing out sweetmeats willy-nilly
Overall loveliness
Laundry
Laundry + local area
How long does laundry usually take?
Unhappiness with laundry service
Best complaint procedures + laundry
Lodging protests with local laundry guilds
Trying to understand the insistent unfairness of certain
    laundry owners
Getting refunds
Demanding refunds
Aggressively demanding refunds
Small claims court

Unjust small claims court decisions
Revenge
Revenge + gloating launderers
Systems of revenge
Devising entire philosophical systems to mete out
    ruthless revenge
Devious schemes + laundry
Underhand shenanigans + laundry
Devoting the rest of your life to destabilizing corrupt
    washer folk from the top down
Ensuring a legacy
Why do some names become adjectives?

MICHELANGELO

Painting ceilings
How long should it take to paint a ceiling?
Should I cancel my weekend plans + painting ceiling
Average chapel ceiling size
Should I get paid by the square inch?
Good subjects for ceiling paintings
Some lovely ducks + ceiling
Happy man giving a thumbs up + ceiling
Everything I've ever eaten + ceiling
Why do they always want something religious?
Which body parts should be touching + sistine chapel
Bullying Leonardo into inventing a brush on a really
    long pole
Far away paintings + doing a rubbish job?
Padding out the sistine chapel with a few well-rendered
    labradors
Compensation
Am I entitled to workplace compensation?
Workplace compensation + enormous neck cricks
Chronic back ache + fresco
Repetitive stress injury + God's finger
Why are Popes such dicks?
Chasing up invoices + slippery popes
If I sue the Pope will I go to hell?
Do architects make more money than painters?
Do architects get more tail than painters?
Do people with one name get paid more?
Good things to paint
Something with Jesus in it?
Bearded figures around a table?

Lady with one knocker hanging out for no discernible
    reason?
Good names for sculptures of people called David
Getting blokes called David to stand still for five
    bloody minutes
How to sculpt realistic wangs
Good terms for a man living during the renaissance
    who is brilliant at loads of stuff
What is a basilica?
Is a basilica some kind of
    lizard thing?
Why would the church want
    me to make a lizard thing?
Getting popes to stop calling
    you Mike
Raphael + Leonardo +
    possible vigilante
    group?

JUST THE CEILING LEFT TO DO, MIKE. YOU OK WITH THAT?

LUCREZIA BORGIA

Relationships
How to form relationships
Relationships for lazy people
Relationships for really lazy people
How can I meet someone without leaving the house?
How can I meet someone without leaving the room I
    share with my brother?
Brotherly love + definition
How to make family get-togethers really awkward
Hot siblings in my very local area
Effective ways of dumping close family members
Avoiding confrontation
Avoiding confrontation via poisoning
Suitable gifts for dads who also happen to be popes
Fancy slippers?
Expensive aftershave?
A quick bunk up?
Should I become a nun?
Should I bang a bunch of nuns?
Suitable finger food + orgy
Suitable poisoned finger food + orgy
Upsides to incest
Why are the Medicis so lame?
Rumours to spread about the Medicis
The Medicis are secretly satanists
The Medicis perform bizarre acts with donkeys
The Medicis are all entirely hairless
How to get my body renaissance ready
Looking good in frescos
Have I got a crush on Barthélemy d'Eyck?

Barthélemy d'Eyck pictures
Barthélemy d'Eyck nudes
Barthélemy d'Eyck + girlfriend?
Barthélemy d'Eyck + girlfriend + poisoning?
How to be alluring when it takes you four-plus hours
    to get this dress off
How to be alluring when we're all riddled with cysts
How to be alluring when everyone smells massively
    of dung
Getting it on while a lute plays in the background
Why is continual ruthless plotting so exhausting?
Ruthless plotting shortcuts
When is it my turn to be pope?
I can just do that thing where I beg for forgiveness on
    my deathbed, right?

MARTIN LUTHER

Names
Why is my name two first names?
Why is my name two rubbish names?
What were my parents thinking?
How could my parents hate me so much?
Famous people with two first names
Non-lame famous people with two first names
Being made fun of for having two first names
Why does everyone pick on me for having two first names?
Why do people pick on me more than that kid completely
    covered in hair?
Great new names
'Martin Hammerplunge'?
'Marty De Sexlady'?
'M-Dog Shamalam'?

Would adding 'King' to the end make my name better?
Did I have a dream?
Why won't my parents let me add King to the end?
Why are my parents so evil?
Praying to God for a name change
Praying harder to God for a name change
Why isn't God listening to my prayers?
Hating God
Hating God and my parents
Pleading with Popes for name change
Hating Popes
Hating Popes and God and my parents
Revenge
Revenge on popes and God and my parents and all those
    nasty boys at school
Theology
Studying theology purely out of spite
Disrupting religion for vengeful purposes
What's the best way of distributing a pamphlet?
Do I really have to trudge about handing pamphlets out
    or can I just nail one somewhere?
Basic hammer use
Holding the entire Catholic Church to ransom
Kickstarting the Protestant Reformation in lieu of
    name change
Can I just change my name?
Do I really not need any permission for a name change?
Desperate religious back-pedalling
Best apology card for popes
Does God bear a grudge?
Creating a schism between protestants and catholics +
    any repercussions?

HENRY VIII

World records
How to break world records
World records + kings
World records + kings + girth
World records + king + wives
World records + king + wives + slaughtering
Great big turkey leg + delivery
Slimming birds of prey + arm
Male beard maintenance + venison chunks
How to talk to women
How to talk to women from Aragon
Breaking bad news
Breaking bad news to women from Aragon
Best outsized hats with feathers
Treating equine hernias
Greensleeves + my jam
Pissing off catholics
How to set up a new christianity branch
How to set up a new christianity branch + overheads
Convincing people that a new christianity branch won't
    have any drawbacks
Good names for new christianity branches
'Henry's Church'?
'New Church of Good Times'?
'Church of Catholics Suck'?
Techniques for convincing people we should leave the
    Church of Rome
We'll have 350 million pieces of gold a week to spend on
    our own religion + believable?
Suitable condolence gifts for Popes

Suitable condolence gifts for Kings of Spain
Fruit Baskets + bulk buy?
Mary Rose hire
Best ways to stop ships sinking
How Tudor am I?
Things marriage guidance counsellors like to hear
Definition of misogynist
World record + misogyny
What is a 'Cleeves'?
How to talk to women from Cleeves
Breaking bad news to women from Cleeves
Name: Catherine + fetish?
Positive spin + beheadings
Good rhymes for remembering spouses

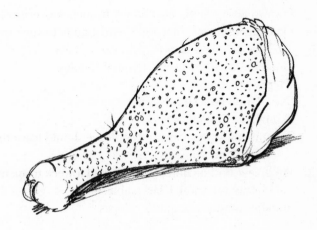

NOSTRADAMUS

What should I do with these discarded prophecies?

'Two clumsy brothers will carry ladders and chuckle'

'Trolls will be become real'

'Every four years people will debate endlessly about
    whether a doctor should be possibly black or a woman'

'There will be eleven hundred different types of yoga, each
    more expensive than the last'

'Man will travel to the moon for a period of about four
    years and then forget all about it'

'Idiots will buy very chunky chronographs to wear on
    their wrists'

'Despite it not being a concern for millennia, suddenly no
    one will be allowed pubic hair'

'A really creepy heavy bejewelled yellow-headed man will
    turn out to be really creepy'

'Man will fly but too many kids will ruin it'

'Six friends will frequent a local coffee merchant and one
    will say "could it be more . . ." quite a lot'

'An old lady will put a cat in a bin'

'Kale will be like so big right now'

'Colourful drawings will appear on the skin of every man
    and trashy woman'

'Velcro will be a thing'

'We will all laugh at the haircuts and trouser styles of the
    previous generation'

'A scotsman and a tiny woman dressed as a small boy will
    horrify the land with their sexual admissions'

'Man will possess the ability to travel and live in all nations
    but then insist that the people of those nations don't do
    the same'

'A song about a great
   future metropolis
   will be sung at the
   end of weddings'
'A large terrifying floating
   head in the sky will
   provide up-to-the-minute
   wagering information'

'The fate of a continent will be decided by trenches'
'Man will invent a magical box with moving pictures and
   then other men will pretend that they don't own one'
'Pretty much everyone good will all die at once in the
   early 2000s'
'A man with a comical moustache will either try to
   conquer the world or do a funny dance with some
   baked potatoes on forks'
'There won't be any particularly great innovations in
   breakfast foods for ages'
'You'll reach an age where the only thing people will talk
   about is property'
'Caffeinated drinks shall become needlessly complicated'
'All street musicians will become louder and worse'
'Eggs will be good for you then kill you and then be good
   for you again'
'Every street in the land will possess a gambling house
   next to an emporium that sells hot chickens'
'A scarecrow with the head of a pumpkin will almost
   certainly bring about the end of the world'
'Man will have access to all the world's knowledge
   instantly at his fingertips and it will make everyone
   really unhappy'

ELIZABETH I

Shortcuts to reigning
Good queens to base your reign on
Any queens to base your reign on
Where all my queens at?
Is my ruff too big?
Should I trim my ruff?
Do boys like a big ruff or a neat and tidy ruff?
Do I have daddy issues + multiple beheadings
Why do I keep finding old discarded turkey legs in the
    royal bedchamber?
Which one was my mum again?
Effective ways to describe a sovereign's body
Why do they always paint me looking bald?
Executing portrait artists + legality

Good drinks to accompany cousin's execution

What's the best country to pick on when you're sick of picking on France?

How to secretly cop-off with earls when everyone's always staring at you

Why are people always talking about my regina?

Words to describe lots of boats at once

Raleigh + Drake + which one's which?

Quitting tobacco

Quitting potatoes

Things to talk about that aren't boats

Best capes for puddle jumping

What's the deal with those long trumpets with flags hanging off them?

Being more bawdy

Why are all our dances so slow and boxy?

Interesting things to say when visiting plague victims

Good nicknames for lady monarchs

'Her Vagesty'

'The Lizbian'

'No Dick Magilacuddy'

Is there any chance I can go to the theatre and not see a Shakespeare play?

Basic sex tips

Really basic sex tips

Birds + bees

Soothing regal bee stings

Soothing regal beak wounds

Why are they always calling me a virgin + I'm the queen for god's sake

What do I do if my Elizabethan period is late?

GALILEO

Convincing excuses for staying out all night + wife
Nocturnal bird watching?
Brass rubbing after dark?
Stargazing?
Stargazing for beginners
Stargazing for adulterers
Stargazing for convincing wives that you're stargazing
    and not up to anything shifty
How come I'm rubbish at knowing people's star signs?
Which one is the moon?
Is Venus just going through a phase?
Is there some sort device that helps you look at
    faraway things?
Magical looking tube?
Good name for magical looking tubes
'The Magical Looking Tube'?
'The Cylinder of Neary Far'?
'The Closeupinanimator'?
'Rod of Sight'?
'The Voyeur's Delight'?
'Telescope'?
Officially, what is the best end of a telescope to
    look into?
Can I use telescopes to look at girls?
Battling accusations of peeping
Subtle ways to rip off Copernicus
Uses for a nearby leaning tower
Dropping things from a nearby leaning tower
Dropping things from a nearby leaning tower for science
Dropping things from a nearby leaning tower for a laugh

Winning lawsuits connected to dropping things from a
    nearby leaning tower
Why kids shouldn't stand under nearby leaning towers if
    they don't want things dropped on them by geniuses
How bad could an inquisition be?
Things the Earth might revolve around
Things the Earth might revolve around that won't make
    popes shout at you
Astronomical u-turns
Scientific back-pedalling
Nice things that Popes like
How to do the fandango

PERHAPS THE EARTH REVOLVES AROUND THIS WOMEN'S BATH HOUSE?

SHAKESPEARE

How to do dead good writings
Doing stories that people like and that make loads of sense
Elizabethan baldness cures
Average number of gentlemen in Verona
Danes
What sort of Danes should I write about?
Great Danes?
Sad Danes?
Sad Danes + commercial potential
Sad Danes + musical?
'To be or not be too?'
Hunchback kings + what things would they trade their
    kingdom for?
Kingdom trade + sweets?
Kingdom trade + another better kingdom?
Kingdom trade + a less lumpy back?
Why are so many pubs named after my head?
Dickish things Scottish people do
How to prove you wrote your own plays
Which English towns have the largest concentration of
    merry wives?
How many kings called Henry have there been?
What's the best part of Henry IV?
Getting monarchs to like you
Elizabethan rug merchants
'To be or I literally couldn't give a toss mate'
Easiest small mammals to tame
Creepy plays about kids that kiss
Dickish things donkeys do
Emperors obsessed with salad

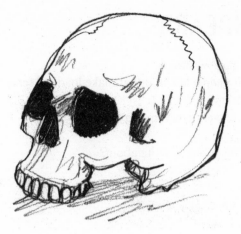

How to lose your Midlands accent
Best season to compare women to
Are Moors trustworthy?
'To be or not really that bovved'?
Why are so many pubs named after my arms?
What deadly pets do Egyptians have around?
Cheap skull rental + Southwark area
Most interesting number for a night
Bawdy serving wenches in my area
Ending scenes with bears in a non-ludicrous way
Dickish things pucks do
Elizabethan toupee artisans
Best time of year to have a dream
'To be or moving back in with Anne Hathaway'?
What is the legal definition of comedy?

GUY FAWKES

How to #TakeBackControl
Best way to send politicians very quickly upwards in bits
Subtle names for plots
Best snacks for plotting meetings
Are dips appropriate at plotting meetings?
Boy, how great is the Pope?
Appalling pseudonyms + John Johnson
How to get your pseudonym changed
Convincing fellow plotters that your pseudonym is
    really crap
Pseudonym appeals process
Am I on the right side?
Invoicing for mass murder
Should I get paid up front?
How to build a tunnel
How to build a tunnel in the right direction
How to build a catholic tunnel
Health and safety basics + eviscerating royalty
What should we replace parliament with?
A catholic theme park?
A massive confessional?
A large smouldering crater?
Looking nonchalant while carrying large amounts of
    explosives into public buildings
Best buckled hat to wear + parliamentary atrocities
Hilarious things to say when captured
'Stick a Fawkes in me, I'm done!'
'What? This gunpowder? Oh, that's just for my own
    personal use'
'I'm not the Guy you're looking for!'

Funny last meal requests

Blaming others + treason

Could I get it reduced to 'not quite so high treason' on appeal?

What does the drawn bit in hung, drawn and quartering involve?

Does someone actually draw me?

What happens to the drawings afterwards?

Insuring your head will look great on a pike

Months that rhyme with 'remember'

How to fulfil a lifelong dream of becoming a recurring effigy

DON QUIXOTE

Cheap armour for the insane
Convincing people your first name isn't donkey
Good designs for heraldic crests
Box of frogs proper beneath many bananas
A phalanx of loons astride an azure nut
A loosened screw atop a cuckoo atop a fruitcake
How portly should my sidekick be?
What would be a good name for my lance?
La Mancha + gender + musical?
Directions to the nearest imaginary giant
Is that big bloke with four arms waving at me?
How to pick fights with random peasants
How to pick fights with random musketeers
How to pick fights with random farm machinery
Best agricultural architecture to attack
Plough + pincer movement
Dibber + punching
Hayloft + rearguard action
Sword sharpening for the mentally unstable
Best fruitless romantic gesture
Horse mounting techniques for the elderly
Equine core exercises
Convincing Sancho to clean his ass
Am I more gangly or lanky?
Cut-rate saddles for crazies
Styling out glaring chivalrous mistakes
Would this make a good book?

FAUST

What should I mention at my meeting with Satan?
His lovely outfit?
Terms and conditions?
Small print?
Grace periods?
Any hidden costs?
Relocation packages
Do I get my soul back at the end?
Does it hurt when my soul is removed?
How and where will my soul be stored?
Do I need to bring my own towels + hell
Will I be eligible for any sort of upgrade + hell
Signing in blood + queasiness
My affinity for goats
What shouldn't I mention at my meeting with Satan?
His horns?
What his favourite colour is?
What that smell is?
If he has any kids
If there's a Mrs Satan
Dante or Milton
Angels?
The whole God area in general?
If Beelzebub is a different person?
The word 'damn'
Getting the pact named after you rather than him
My plan to use a fake soul made from plywood

ISAAC NEWTON

Apples
Bastard apples
Bastard stupid apples
Why do apples fall?
Why do apples fall on me in particular?
Revenge
Apple revenge
Made-up invisible forces + apple revenge
Good names for made-up invisible forces
'Isaacness'?
'Newtonology'?
'Droppy Down Down Good'?
Why are apples so stupid?
Making things sound 'sciencey'
Convincing scientific statements
Convincing scientific statements + enormous
    powdered wig
Sundials + erotic
Secretly destroying the work of scientific rivals
Publicly destroying the work of scientific rivals
Chatting up birds with maths
Rudimentary telescope
Rudimentary telescope + uses
Rudimentary telescope + saucy uses
Rudimentary telescope + apple revenge
Motion
Theories of motion
Theories of motion + super sexy
Why are all other scientists so crap?
Why are all other apples so crap?

Alchemy
Alchemy + real?
Alchemy + meeting lovely ladies
Alchemy + elementary sexbot
Self-promotion
Self-promotion + rivals
Self-promotion + crushing rivals
Self-promotion + crushing apples
Should I start a cider business?
Apples + booooooooo

HAZEL BADWYFFE, WITCH

Cheap newt eyes + local area
Why are my teats always so cold?
Descaling a cauldron
Is a Witchfinder General like an
    army guy or just a non-specific Witchfinder?
Cat allergies + irony
How to get your nose its wartiest
Should I wear my pointy hat to my trial?
Isn't calling it a witch trial a bit of a giveaway?
Why is it called a ducking stool when it's obviously more
    of a chair?
Words that rhyme with hubble
How to + cackling + videos
Broomstick flying + preventing bugs flying into your mouth
Would a dustpan fly in a pinch?
Is it always the witching hour for me?
What's the difference between a pentagram and a pentangle?
Does adding a K to the end of 'magic' make it more spooky?
Why does everything have to happen at night and in the
    woods?
Tricking stupid virgins with apples
Freaking out Christians for LOLs
Good term for being the victim of some kind of hunt
    against orthodoxy
Why are they called spells + my dyslexia + trigger warning
How can I go from hag to WAG?
Planning permission + gingerbread dwellings + non-
    traditional construction

Is Halloween too commercial these days?
Avoiding Wiccans

CINDERELLA

PTSD
Could I have PTSD?
PTSD + recent balls
Did I really go to a ball?
Why would I go to a ball?
Do I think I went to a ball in a vegetable?
Am I having a nervous breakdown?
Where did all my clothes go?
Rags + midnight + public nudity laws
Did I inhale too much carpet cleaner + domestic servitude
What the hell did I do to my dog?
Complicated hallucinations + supposed godmothers
Step-siblings + physical deformities
Why can't I remember my dad?
Is Cinderella really my name?
What does my name mean?
I thought my name was Yvonne
Why would royalty base an entire relationship on footwear
     + possible schizophrenia
Brain tumour + symptoms
If this is all in my head, what was I dancing with?
Is the man at the door really a prince or just some local
     weirdo?
Why does it feel like my whole life is a pantomime?
Why call it a slipper when it's obviously a mule?

SAMUEL JOHNSON

Words
Trying to put words in the right order
Trying to put words in exactly the right order
Trying to put words in exactly the right order to a
    ludicrous degree
Trying to put words in exactly the right order to a
    ludicrous degree + could I actually have a disorder?
Could words collected together in some sort of book be
    a thing?
Could words collected together in some sort of book be
    a money-spinner?
Apt name for wordy collection tome
'Book of rampant written down-ness'?
'Things you tend to say-onary'?
'The Stuff-ocator'?
'Mr Johnson's great big fun book of bumper words'?
'Honest Sam's guide to looking things up'?
Calling yourself a doctor when you're not really one
    + legality
Preventing people in taverns from showing you their rash
Best way to list words
Sexiest ones first?
By number of vowels?
Just the ones I like?
Is it OK to put 'Samuel Johnson (noun) – The Best'?
What does definition mean?
How can I find out what definition means?
Do I really have to do all the words?
What about words people already know the meaning of
    like buns or cat flap?

How often can I stick in 'no need to explain, we all know
    what a windmill is'
Cities to avoid when you're tired of life
Boswell
Who is Boswell?
Where is Boswell?
Is Boswell stalking me?
Why does Boswell keep asking me about synonyms for 'fat'?
Is it Boswell who keeps underlining the word corpulent in
    my dictionary?
How to stop Boswell calling you Sammo Jammo all
    the time
Will my dropsy eventually cancel out my gout?
Sequels to the dictionary
'Dictionary 2: Word Up'?
'Dictionary 3: Things That Sound a Bit Like Words
    But Aren't'?
'Dictionary 4: Diction After Dark'?

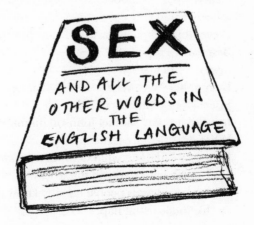

CASANOVA

I'M RUFFLED, FOR HER PLEASURE

How to say 'You are a sexy lady'
   in Spanish

How to say 'Did you sit in a pile
   of fondant? Cause you have a
   pretty sweet derriere' in Latin

How to say 'Can I have
   directions? TO YOUR
   PANTALOONS' in Thai

How to say 'You must be aspic,
   cause fruited preserves don't
   shake like that' in Polish

How to say 'At what hour do you
   have to be back in heaven?'
   in Bengali

How to say 'Was your dad agriculturally aligned? Because
   you have great melons' in Swiss

How to say 'Did you travel from the Orient? Because I'm
   gonna get in Ja-panties' in Japanese

How to say 'I've got a duomo dome looking for a home'
   in Dutch

How to say 'Is your father a baker perchance? Because
   your buns are awesome' in Swiss

How to say 'Are you an orphanage? As I want to give you
   kids' in Nepalese

How to say 'My chirurgeon says I'm lacking Vitamin U'
   in Serbian

How to say 'Have you been to the alienist lately? Cause I
   think you're lacking some Vitamin Me' also in Serbian

How to say 'Excuse me, but I do believe I may have
   dropped something. LIKE MY JAW!' in Balinese

How to say 'My love for you is like dysentery, as I just can't hold it in' in Irish

How to say 'Are you Jewish? Cause you ISRAELI HOT' in Hebrew

How to say 'Are you African? Because afri-I-can if you can baby' in African

How to say 'Are you Australian? Because you meet all of my koala-fications' in Australian

How to say 'Have you been chased by gentlemen on horseback lately, because you are such a fox' in English

How to say 'If I had a groat for every damsel I've seen as beautiful as you, I'd have a single groat' in Arabic

How to say 'Someone contact a pontiff, as heaven is missing an angel' in Peruvian

How to say 'If I could rearrange the alphabet, I would put U and I together (if those letters exist in your language)' in Berber

How to say 'I must be in the Uffizi, because you truly are a work of art' in Coptic

How to say 'You must be Jamaican, because Jamaican me crazy' in Jamaican

How to say 'Is your papa Guy Fawkes? Because you are the bomb' in Chinese

How to say 'Is your last name Mozart, because I can't compose myself' in Icelandic

How to say 'Didn't I see you on the cover of *The Ladies' Fashionable Repository*?' in Congolese

How to say 'I'll be going down in history, but I'll go down on you first' in Welsh

How to say 'Wow! Are those real?' in Catalan

GEORGE WASHINGTON

Cherries
Eating cherries
Trying to eat cherries with wooden teeth
Why are the delights of cherries denied to the wooden-teeth wearer?
Stupid cherries
Stupid cherries and the crappy trees they grow on
Why are cherry trees so dumb?
Destroying cherry trees
Revenge on cherry trees
Harnessing political power to admonish cherry trees
Crossing the Delaware to avoid cherries
Effective poses to strike while crossing the Delaware
How to stand still in a boat for long periods
Looking glum in portraits
Thinking about cherries + portraits
How can I get me some of that 'continental congress'?
British weak points
British + overly stewed tea?
British + overt sexual references?
British + references to improper dentistry?
Do the British love stupid cherries?
Good ways to start constitutions
'We the foxy'?
'We the non-demonstrative slave owners'?
'We the cherry haters'
Constitution + which amendment are we up to?
Constitution + possible future misunderstandings
Constitution + maybe clarify the bit about guns?

Should we make it clear amendments can be amended
    later or is the clue in the name?
Constitution + amendment + fruit
How to look taciturn on money
Memorable sobriquets for legendary leaders
'Daddy of All the American Laddies'?
'Uncle of the Whole Carbuncle'?
'The Pop at the Top'?
Shoehorning masonic symbols into absolutely everything
Shoehorning anti-cherry rhetoric into absolutely
    everything
Can we get that creepy eye/pyramid thing on the flag?
Can Presidents pass laws about fruit?
How to look gloomy on stamps
Am I the state or the city?
Is that monument supposed to be my dick?
Did any other historical figure hate fruit?

MOZART

Am I too precocious?

Does the fact that I know what precocious means prove
   that I'm too precocious?

Do most child stars enjoy happy fulfilling lives?

Should I call myself Mozzer?

Am I basically eurotrash?

Composing basics

Best note to go after G

Definition of minuet + is it like a really small minute?

Are oboes really necessary

How do you pronounce fugue?

Tunes excitable dandies really dig

Should I be getting paid per crotchet?

Salieri + hilarious tricks

Fake poo + Salieri

Fake springy snake in biscuit tin + Salieri

Laxative in claret + Salieri

Going on tour

Getting me some tour strange

Getting girls to perform on my magic flute

Getting girls interested in my horn section

Getting girls to eine kleine my nachtmusik

Good tour merchandise

Mozart branded oversized pantaloons?

Extra-fancy candelabra with my profile on it?

Piano key cravat?

Should I upgrade to one of those tour carriages with the
   bunk beds in the back?

When do groupies start?

Music that will sound good in a merchant's hall

Music that will sound good in an apothecary waiting room
Music that will sound good while calling a futuristic
    communication device
Witty quips about fingering
Hilarious banter about holding balls
Truly stupendous one-liners concerning tromboning
Best bits of Figaro's life to write operas about
Figaro's first day at school?
Figaro's small business loan?
The Prom Night of Figaro?
Phoning it in + emperors
Why are people always asking me to rock them?
Dying while writing a requiem + irony
Hilarious facial expressions + death mask

MARIE ANTOINETTE

What is aristo short for?
Queen of France + perks
Which Louis am I marrying?
Roman numeral basics
Loving a man who wears tights
Why don't I have any furniture named after me?
Treating throne sores
Is it possible to suffer from moat envy?
Why don't the vile, filthy underclasses like me?
Trying to appear sympathetic while holding a giant
    bejewelled orb
Why do the rubies keep falling off my gilded carriage
    that I never use?
Where to order champagne glasses in the shape of
    my knockers

Does my name mean I'm a small antoine?
What's the point of my tiny fabric umbrella?
What's fancier, lots of pairs of shoes or one massive shoe?
Best precious stones to blow your nose on
Bulk-buying beauty spots
Finest lead-based bosom powder
French kissing for beginners
Meals that aren't one bird stuffed inside another bird
How did I ever do without someone wiping my arse
    for me?
Getting foie gras stains out of your caviar
How exactly do I poop in this thing + skirt as wide as
    a bungalow?
Are any musketeers not gay?
What is a scarlet pimpernel
How do you catch scarlet pimpernel
Scarlet pimpernel + symptoms
Who gave me scarlet pimpernel?
Things disgruntled peasants eat
Do peasants actually need to eat?
Good jokes about poor people
Good jokes for poor people
Witty things to say to cackling knitting harridans
Disguising an aristocratic accent
Trading powdered wigs for cigarettes in prison
Is Robespierre just a bloke called Pierre with a robe on?
When I ask for mercy why do they keep saying 'you're
    welcome'?
Should I ask for cake as my last meal for a laugh?
Do heads grow back?

HORATIO NELSON

Why does my first name sound like throwing up?
Why are boats girls?
Great names for boats
HMS Floatzilla?
HMS Sea Spanker?
HMS Boatgasm?
Is HMS short for 'Hey, My Ship!'?
'Hello Manly Sailors'?
'Horatio Might Sink'?
What does HMS stand for anyway?
How not to snigger when saying 'frigate'
Keeping sailors entertained
Keeping sailors entertained + non-rude
On-board entertainment options
Flamboyant gentleman behind the pianoforte?
Washed up vocalists of dubious origin
Magical types in possession of many coloured scarves
Getting over a fear of cannons
Did I marry a woman called Fanny just to get a laugh out
      of the other sailors?
What does England expect every man to do?
His trousers up?
Naval gazing + only one eye
How to tell if you're dating a skank
Should the Lady part of Lady Hamilton's name be in
      inverted commas?
Practical sex tips for one-armed men
Should I get a hook?
Should I get an eyepatch?
Am I turning into a pirate?

Disability benefit
Disability benefit + naval
Am I eligible for workplace accident compensation?
How to make your boat go faster than their boat
Big guns
Bigger guns
Biggest guns
Trafalgar + directions
Does it make more sense to avoid
    Charing Cross Road altogether?
Kissing men while dying + tips
Dying kiss + tongue?
What if he doesn't call me
    afterwards?
Why can't they submerge me in
    brandy before I'm dead?
Getting over a fear of heights
    and pigeons

NAPOLEON

Why don't tall girls like me?

Average height + France + 1800s

Would joining the army make me look taller?

Army rank advancement via diplomatic shrugging

Army rank advancement via a series of exponentially
    larger hats

Getting troops to like you

Getting troops to like you when you're very French

Which part of the body do armies march on?

Things that look quite flashy in battle but don't actually
    do anything in particular

Interesting horse names

Would running France make me look taller?

Could I pass a law that makes everyone else a bit shorter?

Sexual rumours + short military leaders

Available widows in the Greater Paris area

Would marrying a widow make me look taller?

Effective phrases for gently dissuading wives and
    mistresses

Signs of infidelity + former widows

Would becoming emperor make me look taller?

How to make an emperor's coronation not look too swish
    + that whole revolution thing

What's the French for 'that escalated quickly'

Will trying to invade everywhere at once cause any
    problems?

Will trying to invade everywhere at once make me
    look taller?

What does pyrrhic mean?

Making all your mates aristocrats on the sly

Good names for heirs
'Napoleon II – The Hunt for Robespierre's Gold'?
'Napoleon III – The One with Mr T'?
'Napoleon IV – The Final Judgement'?
Is it weird to keep naming my kids the same thing?
Is it weird that all my heirs look like that guy who
    delivers the cheese?
Ensuring that really bad campaigns aren't named
    after you
Would invading Russia make me look taller?
How many fronts does Russia have?
What to do in battles when the enemy just keeps running
    away from you
Directions to Moscow
Directions away from Moscow + quickest route?
Things Nelson generally likes to do in battles
Why don't I have any clothing items named after me
    + Wellington
What's a healthy number of times to abdicate?
Days out in Elba
Should I try to make a comeback
Days out in St Helena

BEETHOVEN

Tunes
Original tunes
Has anyone done this one yet: Dum?
Dum Dum?
Der Dum Dum?
Der Dum Dum Dum?
Der Der Dum?
Dum Der Dum?
Der Der Dum Dum Der?
Der Doo Dum?
Doo Doo Dum Dum?
Dum Der?
Dum Dum Der?
Der Dum Doo Dum?
Diddley Dee?
Der Der Der Der Der?
Der Der Der Der Der Der Der Der Der Der Der Der Der?
Managing frustration
Dum Dum Dum Der Der?
Dum Der Der Dum?
Dum Dum Dummy Dum?
Doo Doo Doo Doo Doo?
Der Der Dum Der Doo?
Da Doo Ron Ron?
Ech Ech Ech Ech Ech?
Maintaining focus
Der Dum Dum?
Dum Dum Dum Der?
Dum Der Dum Der?
Der Dum?

Dree Doo Doo?
Doo Doo Dum?
Dum Der Der?
Duuuuuuuuuuuuuuuuuuuuuuuuuuuuuuuuuuuuuuuum?
Retraining opportunities + Vienna area
Dum Dum Dum Dum Dum?
Dum Dum Dum Dum Der?
Der Der?
Der Der Der?
Am I going deaf?

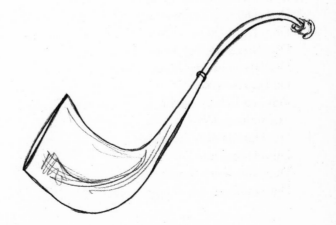

JANE AUSTEN

Research
Should I do more research?
Should I do more sex research?
Writing books about nobs
No, I mean writing books about posh people
Interesting names for leading men
'Bosworth Snootington'
'Fitzsnarkley Nosexfield'
'Colinwendingley Firthpatrickdom'
Is there anything that can't be set in a drawing room?
Why are squires always hitting on me?
How to write in a bonnet
Things that might perk my books up
Action?
Things happening?
Events unfurling at a non-glacial pace?
Hilarious things for women to fall off that sound a bit
    rude + cobbs
Things that people on horses tend to say
Is Northanger Abbey really all that funny even in this
    day and age?
Is north really the angriest direction?
Fun things to do with crinoline
Names of parks in Nottinghamshire
What do single men with a good fortune tend to want
Dirty books?
Chicks with giant racks?
A nice new hat?
Is *Persuasion* a self-help book?
Why do my bodices keep ripping?

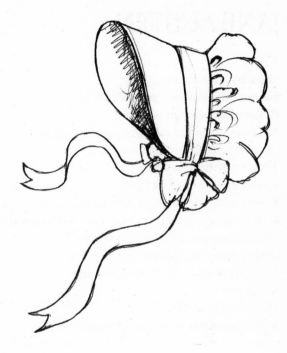

Things sisters say
Things clergy say
Good book titles with pride in them
'Pride and Hating the French'?
'Pride and Priding Monthly'?
'Pride and (In the name of love)'?
Are all novels better when they have the word 'and' in
    the title?
Wait, aren't sense and sensibility basically the same thing?
Did I write *Jane Eyre*?
Is there a way to get my books performed regularly at
    tea-times on Sunday?

LORD BYRON

Shirts
Big shirts
No, you don't understand, REALLY big shirts
Big shirt laundry
Big shirt + general flouncing
Writing poems in a big shirt
Looking after a bear in a big shirt
Fighting duels in a big shirt
Challenging people to duels while wearing a big shirt
How to cheat at duels
Extra-long sword?
Hiding angry midget in big shirt
Shouting 'look at the size of that shirt' at the optimum
    moment
Half-sister + sex + legality
Half-sister + sex + legality + big shirt

Things that women generally walk in?
High heels?
Formation?
Dog poop?
Filthy limericks + money-spinner?
Things that rhyme with gusset
How can someone who's a poet possibly get laid so very
    very much?
How to spell child in a 'poetical' way
Keeping your lovely locks at their flowingest
Great poems about people called Don
Why am I so fertile?
How can I make myself less fertile?
Cold baths + male barrenness
Catching nads on rocks + disrupting sperm count
Thinking about various popes when doing it?
Or should I just carry on banging my sister?
Good epithets for self-description
'Insane, inflamed and quite frequently in Spain'
'Bonkers, stonkers and really good at conkers'
'Nutsy, gutsy and a little bit slutsy'
How many illegitimate children do I need before it
    qualifies as a brood?
How to stop nightmares + Frankenstein + that shizzle
    is scary
Best Mediterranean hotspot + death

LOUIS BRAILLE

Effective language for the blind
Creating a new language for the sightless
Communication techniques for the visually impaired
Shouting?
Really shouting?
Shouting in a funny voice?
Some kind of electrified helmet?
Morse code
Morse code but on a page
Morse code but on a page + lumpy
Do the blind like lumps?
Can the blind understand lumps for some reason?
Should the lumps just spell out the words or be more
    clever than that?
How to spell the word lump in lumps
What should the lumps be made out of?
Lumps + ham?
Lumps + gunpowder?
Lumps + mousetraps?
Would lumps work for the deaf too?
Good name for lump language
'Lumpish'?
'Fingered French'?
'Touchy Feely'?
Would it be egomaniacal to name it after myself?
Would it be awesome to name it after myself?
Expanding braille into other markets
Braille gramophones?
Braille movies?
Some sort of braille Olympics?

Braille catering?

Am I a jerk or should blind people be more grateful?

Should the blind worship me as some sort of god?

Where are all the blind statues to me?

Shouldn't I at least get my own guide dog?

Do I have a thing for blind chicks?

Inventing more languages

Language for the perpetually queasy?

Language for the hefty?

New ways of communicating for those with no sense of
    direction

Is that rash on my neck trying to tell me something?

CHARLES DICKENS

Urchins
What are urchins?
Can urchins read?
Are urchins litigious?
What is gruel?
Is gruel real?
Gruel recipes
How to spell 'gruel'?
Actress ankles
Charles Dickens
'Charles Dickens'
'Charles Dickens' + actress
How to keep affairs secret
Suitable gifts for furious wives
Standard goose measurements
Roughly what sort of thing happens in a workhouse?
Am I allowed to say 'what the dickens'?
Believable surnames
Unnaturally large bustles
Elizabeth Gaskell
Elizabeth Gaskell + sales figures
Elizabeth Gaskell + feet
How do the poor talk?
How do the underclass talk?
How do lowlifes talk?
What is a barrow boy?
Things misers say
Things women say
Believable things women say
What is a normal number of ghosts?

Uncomplicated undergarments
Etchings + overtly bawdy
Am I a gadfly?
Types of houses + not nice
Grim House?
Dour House?
Appalling House?
Huge impractical bicycles
Dorrits + usual size?
Do people really say 'odds bodkins'?
'Charles Dickens'
'Charles Dickens' + bald
'Charles Dickens' + genius
Removing urchin blood from frock coat
Urchin synonyms

ADA LOVELACE

Inventions
Communication inventions
Device for accessing knowledge instantly
Instant knowledge accessor + potential uses
Watching cats fall over?
Picking fights with strangers?
Picking fights with family members?
Picking fights with notable actors of the day?
Sharing images of various meals?
Sharing images of various sunsets?
Sharing images of various body parts?
Being told where to go?
Being told what to think?
Being told how to make pancakes?
Discovering the facts surrounding current events?

BABBAGE JUST GOT PWNED!

Discovering made-up facts about current events?
Watching people commit carnal acts?
Watching animals commit carnal acts?
Watching animals and people commit carnal acts?
Registering your distaste with absolutely everything?
Registering your distaste with very very specific things?
Unearthing the meteorological conditions for places you
    will never go?
Discovering which half-forgotten classmates have married?
Inaccurately finding out what ailments you don't suffer from?
Disparaging merchants who deliver their comestibles
    ineffectively?
Transferring large sums of money to African royalty?
Transferring the head of a famous body onto the naked
    body of someone else?
Buying cheap books?
Buying cheap printer's ink?
Buying a cheap product from the Far East that doesn't
    actually exist?
Enjoying moving images portraying men in Eastern
    Europe really hurting themselves?
Partaking in charitable endeavours that will probably kill
    a few people?
Illegally obtaining the latest works of famed troubadours?
Allowing the government of the day to know absolutely
    everything about you?
Allowing the criminals of the day to know everything
    about you?
Allowing the neighbours of the day to know everything
    about you?
Wasting vast amounts of time
I will get the credit all for this, won't I?

CHARLOTTE BRONTË

Sisters
Having too many sisters
Identifying sisters by their tuberculosic coughing
Unsyncing menstrual cycles
Which one of us wrote *Jane Eyre*?
Discrete assassination methods + idiot brother
Efficient masturbation in vicarage bunk-beds
Why *Wuthering Heights* is such a crap book
What exactly is wuthering?
Am I currently wuthering?
How high can the average person wuther?
Fun things to do on moors
Sabotaging the literary careers of siblings
Medway towns to name characters after?
Mr Gillingham?
Mr Strood?
Mr Hoo St Werburgh?
What even is a Branwell?
Vicar's daughters + any new jokes
What does TB stand for?
Washing blood out of handkerchiefs
Parts of the house fires usually occur in
Could one of us be called Pat?
Getting Branwell off the mantelpiece
Best places to be fingered in Haworth
Why is Ann such a dick?
Things to do in the sack with a curate
Why is Branwell so stingy with his laudanum?
Are we a coven?
Which one of us is hottest?

Why *The Tenant of Wildfell Hall* is such a tedious read
Good excuses for avoiding church
Innovative yorkshire pudding recipes
Why is Emily such a little tosser?
Can TB ever be sexually attractive?
Covering up violent blood- and saliva-filled spluttering
Good ways to outlive your sisters
Discounts on mass funerals
Which one am I again?

ABRAHAM LINCOLN

Most confusing way of saying the number 87
Beards + wow factor
Why the long face?
Why the long hat?
Ways to make myself look even taller + headgear
Am I the tallest person on Earth right now?
Should I join the circus?
Would I look less presidential if I wore dungarees all
    the time?
Am I that honest + all those shopliftings
How long do civil wars generally last?
Why are they called civil wars when they don't seem
    that civil?
Best side to be on + civil war
Can I swap sides if things start to look a bit dicey?
Mastering a southern accent just in case
Inventive names for addresses made near Gettysburg
White House + obvious jokes + civil war
Am I the best president?
Presidential rankings
Presidential rankings + achievements
Presidential rankings + height
Am I too PC?
I look quite wood-like, am I made from wood?
Am I made of leather? I am quite leathery
Why can't people ever take a decent photo of me?
Can I blame all these stains on James Buchanan?
Do I ever smile?
How good will my face look on the side of a mountain?
Do I have to go on the end + Mount Rushmore

When can I start calling myself King Abe?
Why being on the lowest currency denomination is a
    good thing
Suppressing skipping-rope rhymes about my alcoholism
How to hilariously frighten vice presidents with sudden
    unexpected proclamations
Effective re-election slogans
'Don't Think, Linc!'?
'Keep Taking the Abe-Lets'?
'Vote For Me – I'm The Least-Racist Person So Far'?
Did we send the Booths a Christmas card?
Cheap theatre tickets

CHARLES DARWIN

Pissing off Christians
Pissing off Christians with monkeys
Evolving
What is evolving?
Am I evolving?
Am I evolving right now?
Did I evolve just then?
Can beards evolve?
Have I had too much coffee?
Annoying papists with baboons
Where do species originate?
Colchester?
Did species originate in Colchester?
Things we might have evolved from
Crepes?
Drapes?
Fire escapes?
Why is research so hard and boring and far away?
Survival of the quickest?
Survival of the longest?
Survival of the dampest?
Why do kangaroos even bother having pouches if they
    won't let you clamber into them?
Should that tortoise be that big or am I having a stroke?
Agitating the devout via orang-utans
Is there a God?
Did I just kill God?
Am I God?
Does the fact that I look like God make me more God?
God lookalike competitions + local area

Should I call myself Chuck D?
Evolutionary purpose of beards + soup eating
Rubbing the pious up the wrong way with gibbons
Why marrying your cousin is so great
Why are all my kids so weird?
George Bernard Shaw lookalike competitions + local area
How to tell someone you don't want to dress up as a
    monkey at a book launch
Can putting a dog and a cat in a sack be considered an
    experiment?
Books about worms + dynamite endings
Getting conversations started + mollusc knowledge
Upsetting Unitarians with gorillas
Why won't my wife let me keep barnacles in the house?
Unnerving Methodists with marmosets
Father Christmas lookalike competitions + local area
Vexing Lutherans with tamarins
Is God going to be mad at me?

KARL MARX

Monopoly
How to win at Monopoly
Why am I so bad at Monopoly?
Why does Engels always beat me at Monopoly?
Basic capitalism
Basic capitalism + Monopoly tips
Surely pooling all the money would be more fun?
Can communism help you win Monopoly?
Can communism help you win any board games?

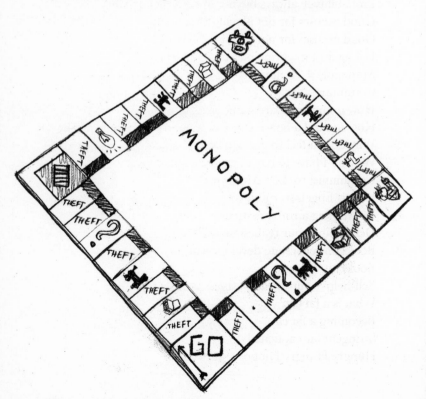

Can communism help you win anything?

How to buy hotels

Cheating at Monopoly

Hiding Monopoly money in large beard

Does the counter you choose make any difference?

Little iron + Monopoly wins

Little dog + Monopoly wins

Little car + Monopoly wins

Which Monopoly counter is the most communistic?

How to tell if someone is cheating at Monopoly

Is Engels a secret capitalist?

Probability + always buying Mayfair before you

Good excuses for not playing Monopoly

Good excuses for not winning Monopoly

Is it against my principles to play Monopoly?

Monopoly + communist version

Communopoly?

How to fund a board game prototype

How to fund a board game prototype + communistically

Why does it feel so good to be the banker?

Why do I have to pay to get out of jail?

Communist tricks + Monopoly

Why is Engels so ruthless?

Developing a ruthless streak

Developing your real estate skills

Books on real estate development

Books on winning

Self-help + cut-throat business practices

What is a fat cat?

Becoming a fat cat

Stringent fat-cat denial

Hungry Hungry Hippos + proletariat

QUEEN VICTORIA

Injecting excitement into long-term relationships
Injecting excitement into regal long-term relationships
Injecting excitement into regal long-term relationships
    with a German
Pneumatic sexual devices
Steam powered pessaries
Clockwork sex eggs
Spinning Jenny + filthy purposes
Gas clamps
Erotic prognosticator
Ribbed orb and sceptre
Agricultural machinery + titular kneading
Humpiograph
Automated bodice ripper
Coal-fired vacuum pump
Apparatus for the heightening of bodily humours
Mechanical peekaboo bussle
Penny farthing + naughty saddle
Shire horse + mild indecency
Pistonical phallicated interrupter
Self-lubricating stableboy
Dredge shaft
Rotary lewdness
Dirigible + nether regions
Edible pantaloons
Propulsive nipple adornments
Those things you pump up and down on railway tracks
'Versuche über Pflanzenhybriden'
Dynamo-electric galvanic restiffinator
A large collection of soothing balms

MADAME BOVARY

L'affair
L'affair discrete
L'affair discrete + garçon du jiggy jiggy
Les underpants érotique
Voulez vous coucher avec moi?
Ce soir?
Parler sale
Voulez vous fricassée mon pompidou?
Les negligee avec peekaboo
Se raser mon fou fou?
Dabble dans mon pamplemousse
Une chaise cheval pour un trop gros homme?
Maison pour un bunk-up dans area locale?
Technique + les kissing avec ici?
Mon peccadillos + trouser baguette + hayloft
Ou est mon petit homme dans le bateau?
L'oignon + aphrodisiaque?
Une kinqué beret pour la sac du testiclé
Hoh-hee-hoh-hee-hoh + ooh la la + zut alors!
Une grande chaise longue pour la rumpeaux
Quest-ce que le chien style?
Manual au position soixante-neuf?
Est ce marriage dans un cul de sac?
Est mon derriere trop gros dans ce?
Souffle romantique sur mon bon bons?
Décolletage + voila!
Suis-j'une femme de la nuit?
Qu'est-ce que le blemish sur mon area privée?

FLORENCE NIGHTINGALE

Establishing a personal brand
Establishing a personal brand with homeware
The lady with the cheese grater?
The lady with the mangle?
The lady with the cutlery drawer?
Memorable affectations
Memorable affectations + illumination
Chick with the wick?
The dame with the flame?
Torch Ho?
Would a lamp help define my nursing career in some way?
Lady of the lamp + trademark
Lady of the lamp + merchandise
Lady of the lamp tea towels?
Lady of the lamp hair rollers?
Lady of the lamp lamps?
Job lot of lamps + cheap
Getting loads of lamps monographed quickly
Other lamp-based avenues
Lamp, The Musical?
Rhythmic words that rhyme with lamp
Catchy songs about lamps
'The Oily Bird Gets the Burn'?
'Give My Lamp a Rub You Tinker'?
'Lamp Vamp Rhumba'?
Learning to tap-dance
Learning to do the splits
Learning to hold a lamp and sing at the same time
What should I do after my musical is a massive success?
Writing life stories?

Good names for autobiography
'Lample Bosom'?
'You Go Flo!'
'You Can't Make a Heroine Without Morphine'?
'Nursed Back to Wealth'?
'Angel of Death: My Confession'?
Should I pop back to the hospital and do a bit of
     nursing eventually?

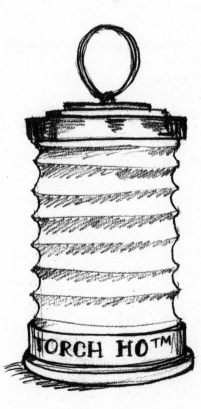

JACK THE RIPPER

How to murder prostitutes
How to murder prostitutes and not get caught
How to murder prostitutes and not get caught despite
    really obvious clues
How to be a minor member of the royal family (and a
    murderer)
How to be a secret minor member of the royal family
    (and a murderer)
Or am I the pope (and a murderer)?
Or just a murderer (and a murderer)?
Committing various atrocities in a top hat
Basic slaughtering in a cape
Advanced moustache twiddling
Effective skulking in shadowy Victorian doorways

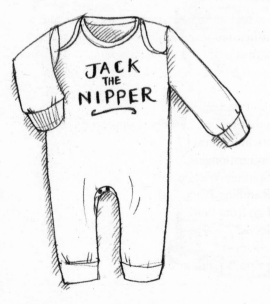

JACK
THE
NIPPER

Low guttural menacing laughs

Why is it so foggy all the time?

Is fog good for covering up murders?

How can I possibly defend myself against a police force armed with whistles?

Bigger whistles + arms race

Good murdering names + Jack

'Jack the Murderer'?

'Jack the Stabber'?

'Jack the Daggerer'?

What hacky sounding words rhyme with Jack?

Dictionary definition + 'rip'

Controlling unquenchable lust at the sight of a table leg

Why are women so provocative with their bare ankles and their unclothed backs of necks?

Am I a murderer or could I just be really clumsy around prostitutes?

Ways to ensure actual murder of actual people becomes a kind of light-hearted romp and people go on walking tours of where you did the actual murders

Perfect ways to start letters to the police + murderer?

'Hello boys!'

'Dear Incompetent Peelers'

'Firstly, don't bother to look for fingerprints on this thing because there aren't any'

Can I frame a costermonger?

Can I frame a Spinney-Wicklagger?

Can I frame a Raddling Plancifier?

Where should I go from here?

Jack the Diplodocus?

Jack the Former Ripper?

Jack the Petting Zoo Attendant?

VINCENT VAN GOGH

Launching your career in art
Getting noticed + artist
Should I try a few wacky stunts to get noticed?
Will acting a bit freaky help me to stand out?
Calculating projected sales + art
Double checking projected sales + art
How could I have sold minus paintings?
That would literally mean someone had sold me a
    painting and I didn't notice
Should I change my dealer?
Should I change my career?
How much do tram operators make?
What about the people that do the signs outside pubs?
Better subjects for paintings
Stars?
Flowers?
Fields?
My own severely damaged head?
Hay fever cures + sunflowers
Unusual gifts
Unusual gifts to impress prostitutes
Unusual gifts to impress Dutch prostitutes
Do prostitutes like randomly cut-off body parts?
Ear portions + gift box?
Stemming blood flow
Stemming blood flow and then quickly painting it
Do I have to wear a monocle now + ear damage
Removing highly ungrateful prostitutes from your life
How to get bits of ear back
Does my brother think I'm a mooch?

Should I get a mirror rather than doing all these
    self-portraits?
Are those voices in my head or is it just the bloke
    next door?
Yellow paint + bulk buy
Should I eat paint?
How delicious is paint?
Paint-based recipes
Paint soufflé?
Emulsion over easy?
Whitewash a l'orange?
Crayons as a side dish?
Why won't anyone sit next to me on the bus?
Why posthumous recognition is pretty lame

OSCAR WILDE

Good names for plays
Something with importance in the title?
The Importance of Being Important
The Importance of Being On Time
The Importance of Being Really Sexy
The Importance in Being Regular in Your Bowel
    Movements
The Importance of Being in Possession of a Very
    Complicated Middle Name
The Importance of Being Aesthetic
The Importance of Being Asthmatic
The Importance of Being Allergic to Vaginas
The Importance of Being Able to Get Married Anyway
The Importance of Being Very Successful in Your Pursuits
The Importance of Being a Literary Sensation
The Importance of Being Very Witty Very Quickly
The Importance of Being Able to Crush Dowagers with
    a Single Quip
The Importance of Being Able to Ascertain the Mood
    of Princes
The Importance of Being Up in the Attic (and Finding
    Spooky Portraits There)
The Importance of Being Well Turned-Out
The Importance of Being 'Well Turned-Out' (If You
    Know What I Mean)
The Importance of Being in Possession of Non-
    Traditionally Coloured Flowers
The Importance of Being Flamboyant
The Importance of Being Conversant in Words That
    Have Double Meanings

The Importance of Being Discreet About Where You
    Go To at Night
The Importance of Being Able to Keep Secrets From
    Close Family Members
The Importance of Being Able to Gauge the Relative
    Aptitude of Husbands
The Importance of Being Knowledgable About Beauty
The Importance of Being Destructively Attracted to
    Certain Young Men
The Importance of Being Nice to The Marquis of
    Queensberry
The Importance of Being Forthright in Refuting
    Certain Claims
The Importance of Being Misrepresented in a
    Legal Setting
The Importance of Being Fairly Regretful About
    Bringing Libel Claims
The Importance of Being Able to Explain
    All Those Rent Boys
The Importance of Being Convincing
    to a Judge
The Importance of Being Unfairly
    Treated
The Importance of Being Jailed
    for a Significant Amount of Time
The Importance of Being Unjustly
    Ruined
Maybe something about a
    fan instead?

SHERLOCK HOLMES

Cocaine
Cocaine + holy crapballs
Scoring really great cocaine
Why cocaine is so brilliant
Yeah I'm a great detective yeah + coke
Jobs for awesome people
Jobs for geniuses
Is there a job where you can just stare at people and work
    out everything about them because you're really?
Why John Watson really gets you, you know
Playing the violin really fast
Playing violin fast + current world record?
World records + do they screen for cocaine?
Why Watson is so awesome
Why blow is so awesome
Coming down from cocaine
Dealing with paranoia
Why does Watson hate me?
Why am I so itchy?
Taking a break from cocaine
Boredom
Cocaine
Cocaine dealers + Baker Street area
YEAH COKE YEAH
Am I autistic or just really high on coke?
Does coke cause autism?
Are crimes committed by giant dogs or is it just the coke?
Adding more awesome amazing flaps to a hat
Smoking loads of pipes at once + coke + OH BOY
Oh God Oh God Oh God have I done too much cocaine?

Symptoms of overdose
Should this stuff be coming out of me?
Why cocaine is evil
Cocaine abusers support groups
Healthy living + detectives
Making a clean go of it
New year + new you
Boredom
Cocaine
Speedy cocaine dealers + Baker Street area
Is all this coke making me constipated + appropriate
    catchphrase

SIGMUND FREUD

Wangs

Ways to trick people into talking about their wangs

Professions dedicated to tricking people into talking
about their wangs

Wang inspector?

Male prostitute?

Some kind of doctor for people who like talking about
their wangs?

Mothers

Ways to trick people into talking about their mothers

Ways to trick people into talking about their mothers'
wangs

Catchy names for analysing neuroses

'Crazy Talk'?

'Mind Boggling'?

'It Probably Means You're Gay'?

People describing dreams + how to make interesting

What's it called when you accidentally say the wrong word
and it's revealing of something deeper

PEANUTS ENVY

A Freudian blooper?

A Freudian whoopsie?

A Sigmund silly?

'Freudian slip' + copyright

'Freudian slip' + high concept gameshow

'Freudian slip' + bespoke lingerie

Making money from crazy people

Making money from crazy people + book idea?

Crazy people + newsreel funnies

'Sigmund Freud and his band of wacky pals'

'Captain crazy and the bonkers bunch'

'Beardo weirdo and his gaggle of deeply damaged people'

What furniture do crazy types like to lie on?

Cheap couch rental + Vienna

Couch stain removal + Vienna

Siggy + good nickname?

Famous Siggys

Dr Siggy?

Getting t-shirts printed

Disguising large foreheads

Why smoking this great big cigar doesn't signify anything

Do I have sex on the brain?

Do I have sex on the couch?

Insulting names for Carl Jung

'Carl Junk'?

'Carl Not-Particularly-Well-Hung'?

'Carl Bunghole'?

What does a recurring dream about a giant couch chasing
    you mean?

Repressing the urge to say 'you so crazy!' to certain people

Everyone knows that I'm just kidding with all this stuff,
    right?

EMMELINE PANKHURST

Booths
Voting
Voting booths
Accessing voting booths
What does the inside of a voting booth look like?
What does the inside of a voting booth smell like?
Going to extreme lengths to equate yourself with
    voting booths
What do men do in booths?
Are there special prizes in booths?
Are there overly cute animals or delicious treats in booths?
Why do I find voting booths so alluring?
Is voting fun?
Sating voting booth curiosity + political movements
Good names for political movements
'Votes For Vag Holders!'

'Electile Dysfunction'

'The Big Hat and Massive Sash Party'

Is purple really my colour?

Ways that ladies can attach themselves to railings

What things can you chain yourself to other than railings?

Chains + luxury items you'd really like

Chains + lovely cream cakes

Chains + the man who works in the off-licence

Am I into bondage now?

Commercial Suffragette merchandise

Suffragette oven gloves?

Suffragette mangle?

Suffragette 'make your hubby happy' kit?

Why do all the other Suffragettes shoot down my
    great ideas?

Should the franchise only be extended to women?

Votes + pets?

Votes + fictional characters?

Votes + working classes?

Celebrating women's suffrage

Overwhelming joy that women finally have the vote

Overcoming voting booth disappointment

LIZZIE BORDEN

Family vacations
How to survive family vacations
How to avoid family vacations
Escaping the tyranny of a Cape Cod vacation
Telling your parents you don't want to go on vacation
  with them
Why are my parents so unreasonable?
Faking illnesses
Convincing measles spots
Believable coughing fits
How to pretend you have pleurisy
Parental scepticism + unfairnessness
Should I run away?
Should I hide under the bed?
Should I murder them?
When is murder a bit of an overreaction?
Murder weapons
Nearby murder weapons
Murder weapons I can locate without leaving the house
  or yard
Vacuum cleaner + patricide
Lawn mower + oedipal-style slaughtering
Hose reel + rapidly becoming an orphan
Trying to convince both parents to fall daintily onto an
  axe head
Good songs to muffle parental screaming
Are axes like frying pans and you shouldn't clean them
  after use?
Getting parental blood out of couch covers
Good cleaning services + Massachusetts

Discreet cleaning services +
    Massachusetts
Bribeable cleaning services +
    Massachusetts
Alibis
Watertight alibis
Slightly leaky alibis that will still work in
    these weird times
Keeping axe murders off your CV
Pretending you don't know what axes are
Suing courtroom artists + there's no way I
    look like that?
Contacting Guinness Book of Records + dumbest
    juries in history
Trying not to express extreme surprise at verdicts
Good titles for books about people who aren't murderers
'Who? Me?'
'I'm Allergic to Axe Handles'
'How I Didn't Brutally Murder My Parents but If I
    Did Here's How I Would Have Done It'
Should I open an axe shop?
Should I open a parental-murdering service?
Getting people with skipping ropes to sing songs
    about you
Vacations in the Cape Cod area

BEATRIX POTTER

Rabbits
Good names for rabbits
Good names for really fluffy cuddly rabbits
'Fuzzy Snugglesome'?
'Bunny Bopkins'?
'Hopsy Hopkins'?
Suitable attire for snuggly bunnies?
Adorable little rabbit waistcoat?
Charming bunny bonnet?
Sweet tiny rabbit jodhpurs?
Keeping rabbits at home
Rabbit next-day delivery
Rabbit + noises at night
Where have all these sodding rabbits come from all of
    a sudden?
Rabbits + pest
Rabbits + tunnelling + established base of operations
Murdering rabbits
Effectively murdering rabbits
Hitting rabbits with a spade
Best rabbit poison?
How many times do I need to shoot a rabbit in the face
    until it's dead?
Names for adorable farmyard pals
'Twitchy-Nose Flopsy'?
'Snuggle-Bunny Cuddle-Chops'?
'Sniffly Chuckle Squiggle Toes'?
Throttling thieving rabbits
Crucifying a rabbit as a warning to other rabbits
Washing rabbit brains out of tweed

Delightful adventures for little bunnies
Rabbit hi-jinks + vegetable-patch shenanigans
Gassing warrens + even the babies
Best vicious dogs for tearing rabbits apart
Electrifying rabbits + pain
Cute names for rabbit siblings
'Hopscotch'?
'Flipsy'?
'Bobbletops'?
Quick rabbit-torso recipes
Can you still eat a rabbit if it's been stabbed repeatedly?
Lovely rabbit tea things
Atrocities + rabbit
Enchanting bunny slippers
What stops rabbits screaming?
Captivating leporine ditties
Kicking rabbits up the arse
Wonderful things rabbits get up to
Evil long-eared bastards

WILBUR WRIGHT

What is the purpose of load extension graphs?
Sperry's rule of precession
What elements are required for oscillatory motion?
What criteria are needed for longitudinal statically
    stable craft?
Overcoming yawing motion
How do head- and tailwinds affect airspeed?
Pogo oscillation
Gauging equations of motion
What is the fuel consumption of an aircraft in a
    holding pattern?
Physical mechanisms to transform pressure into velocity
What is the moderate dihedral angle for a low-wing
    airplane?
Accurate weather simulations
Air characteristics variation
Parasitic drag
Fluid mechanics
Conservation of momentum analysis
Name of the figure consisting of a slow revolution around
    longitudinal axis
Converting pressure height to geometric height
Bernoulli's principle
Variable inlet guide vanes

ORVILLE WRIGHT

Inventing the three-feet-high club
Getting wasted while airborne
When can I start hiring trolley dollies?
When can I start banging trolley dollies?
Why is my brother such a massive nerd?
Getting super-hot chicks via aviation
Wowing crowds with surprising loop-the-loops
Sticking some gun mounts on this puppy
Flying really fast to impress girls in cloche hats
Barnstorming + actual barns
Mooning while airborne + legality?
Boners + altitude
Is the sky the same as international waters?
Is there a sky equivalent of mermaids?
Cock fights + cockpit
Flying this puppy to Reno
How can I possibly look so damn good in a flying jacket?
Other total studs called Orville
In-flight movies + really dirty
Scaring the crap out of dumbasses with my boss propellers
If there's grass on the landing strip, lets fly!

MARIE CURIE

Superpowers
How to get superpowers
What to do if I want to fly unaided?
Smashing big boulders with my bare hands
Why does my husband always want to get involved?
Distancing from husband + development of superpowers
Avoiding all his sidekick talk
Why do they keep giving me Nobel Prizes when all I want
    is the ability to leap tall buildings?
Discovering new elements
Good names for new elements
'Bumium'?
'Hardon'?
'Flubber'?
Using new elements in my secret superpower plans
Trying to assimilate in male-dominated laboratories
Teste/test tube jokes?
Holding a couple of bell jars up to my chest?
Waving my two Nobel Prizes in their dumb faces?
Ditching husband + dead weight
Fun things to do with radiation
Radiation + generally wallow around in it
Radiation + fashioning a kooky hat out of it
Radiation as a delicious sandwich filling
Could X-rays ever come in handy?
Are X-rays purely for novelty purposes?
Could X-rays help defeat my perceived super villain
    arch-nemesis?
Getting your husband to stop saying 'there's chemistry
    between us' every five minutes

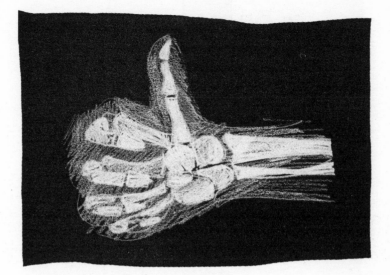

Changing lab locks + husband
Louis Pasteur + single?
Trying to get lab technicians to stop making Polish jokes
    + two Nobel Prizes
Why do I hate kryptonite so much?
Would firing radiation at a hammer then waving it
    around do anything?
Would firing radiation at a spider then getting it to bite
    me do anything?
Would exposing myself to absolutely buttloads of
    radiation do anything?
Will my last name prove to be bitterly ironic?

SCOTT OF THE ANTARCTIC

Snow
What is snow made from?
Why is snow so cold and terrifying?
Do I have a snow phobia?
Is there such a thing as a snow phobia?
Why does opening the fridge make me nauseous?
Why does filling the ice-cube tray cause me to wet myself?
Is sleet evil?
Can snowmen actually come to life?
Abominable snowmen sightings + Esher area
Ways to avoid snow
How to get over a fear of snow
Aversion therapy
Extreme aversion therapy + snow
Extreme aversion therapy + rash expeditions
Convincing unsympathetic loved ones of snow phobia
Convincing unsympathetic loved ones that you're not a wuss
Proving snow phobia to annoying wives via rash expeditions
To defeat snow must one commune with snow?
Are there any closer poles?
Why are Norwegians such arseholes?
Do guns work well against snow?
Flamethrower rental
Are there any ants in the Antarctic?
Hiding in a tent to avoid your crippling fear of snow
How icebergs are my worst fear realized
Why did I do this + living hellscape?
Good things to say when exiting a tent forever

RASPUTIN

Basic hypnosis
How to mesmerize Russian royalty
How to mesmerize Russian royalty and make them think
    they're chickens because that's really funny
Societal advancement via really hard staring
How to get blood out of a shirt
How to get blood out of a small Russian prince
How to stop blood coming out of a small Russian prince
Faking the answers to Bible questions
Are my eyes at their stariest?
Cowls that set off a man's curves
Secreting fabergé eggs + beard
How many fabergé eggs to the rouble?
Do fabergé eggs have fondant inside?
Correct way to eat caviar
Correct way to steal caviar
Sensual vodka cocktails
Erotic things you can do with potatoes
How to look your sexiest in a big fur hat
Painless ways to dump Tsarinas
Man of God + seem to be humping a lot
How to slip your enormous penis into conversation
How to slip your enormous penis into a Tsarina's borscht
Seduction techniques that let you keep your vest on +
    Siberia
Signs you've been poisoned
Signs you've been shot
Signs you're drowning
What are the chances you're experiencing all three at once?
Ranking of greatest love machines + Russian

HARRY HOUDINI

Things to escape from
Paper bag escape?
Wet cardboard box escape?
Milk churn escape?
Where to find milk churns
Do I know anyone who is friends with a farmer?
Do I pour the milk out first?
Ways to pass time in a milk churn
Can crazy eyes and a centre parting be enough of a
    personality?
Would a couple of tigers perk up the act?
Why do locksmiths hate me?
Easy ways to get really slippery very quickly
Really really really small bolt-cutters
Hiding keys in your penile shaft
Storing Allen keys in your anus
Sterilizing Allen keys
Hacksaw blades + prostate
How to stop your job turning into a sex thing
Practical applications for handcuff removal
Why can't I get into the Magic Circle?
Why can't I get into Mary Lou's Magic Circle?
Slipping the phrase 'This is where the magic happens'
    seamlessly into conversations
Why can't I master that balls under the cups thing?
Things to catch in your teeth that aren't bullets
Toothpicks?
Spinach?
Bullet shaped delicious treats?
Should I get a wand?

Do wands really work?
When magicians disappear, where exactly do they go?
Usefulness of glamorous assistants
Do glamorous assistants do more than just point?
Things not to wear on stage + long flowing scarves
Can you rent doves?
How do you stop doves crapping in your top hat?
Do I use the expression 'my hands are tied' too much?
Making my hands slighter
How did my uncle find all those dimes in my ears?
Do I need a catchphrase?
'Now that's escaping!'
'Oh no! I think I left my
    lunch in there!'
'Houdini? Who-doesn't-ni?'
'Who wants to punch me
    in the stomach?'

MATA HARI

Getting started in showbiz
Dead-sexy stage names for dancers
'Sexy Sexington'?
'Hotstuff McKnockers'?
'Slinky O'Dryhumps'?
Why are all the best names taken?
'Manta Ha-Ray?'
'Manatee Harumphs'?
'Baron Hardup'?
Does my name sound a bit like a budget motorcycle?
Seduction techniques
Turn-of-the-century seduction techniques
Provocative foxtrot
Erotic novelty song about bananas?

MATA HARI

ANTI-MATA HARI

Peekaboo cloche hat?
Will men ever hump me for my mind?
Dissuading diplomats from sending you their
    genital etchings
Spying for the fairer sex
Espionage for young ladies
Tit-based traitoring
Which side should I spy for?
Can I spy for both sides + am I just too nice?
Why does everyone think this war is so great?
Trying to cop off with someone who has a truly
    huge moustache
Accessing jodhpurs for romantic purposes
Feigning sexual interest in Belgians
Can I be a courtesan without any legal training?
Disguising a Dutch accent so people will fancy you
Will I ever get a medal for this?
Effective espionage denials
'How did that miniature camera get all up in there?'
'Treason? What, with my back?'
'If it makes you feel any better, I think your side's
    the best'
Does my death sentence mean my burlesque career is
    effectively over?
Clever things to say just before you get shot
'See you all at the after party!'
'You know, I'll be really annoyed if you miss'
'Ah, un gros morte, for a change'
'Not the first time I've had them queuing up to bang me,
    if you know what I mean'

FRANZ KAFKA

Interesting things for fictional characters to turn into
A sideboard
A dinghy
A duck
A dry-cleaner
A pigeon
A pig
A guinea pig
A guinea fowl
A chicken
A cock
A cocked horse
What is a cocked horse?
A horse
A clothes horse
A satanic clothes horse
Two satanic clothes horses
Devils on horseback
A date
A rasher of bacon
A pig
A guinea pig
A hedgehog
A hedge
A hedge sparrow
A satanic hedge sparrow
Some satanic hedge clippers
A possessed lawn mower
A bedevilled compost heap
A devil

Devils on horseback
Dates
Bacon
Pigs
A sausage
A sausage dog
A dog
Dog crap
Flies
A bluebottle
A midge
A load of midges
Too many midges
Someone called Midge
Someone called Madge
Why is this bugging me so much?

> YOUR WRITING,
> IT'S VERY ME-ESQUE.

JAMES JOYCE

The Irish
Being Irish
Faking Irishness
Faking Irishness to make it as a top writer
Basic Irish tropes
What do Irish people do generally?
What kind of things do Irish people say?
Do the Irish like walking around cities aimlessly?
Do the Irish like wakes?
Do the Irish really say 'begorrah'?
Do the Irish tend to say 'top of the morning' instead
    of 'hello'?
Ireland + exact location
Many potato mentions + offensive?
Disguising your lack of Irishness via writing total gibberish
Days out in Dublin + plot
How many times should I mention the Blarney Stone over
    the course of an afternoon?
Authentic sounding names for Irish books
'Limerickians'?
'Dundalkanuts'?
'Corkers'?
Does it ever snow in cemeteries?
Are leprechauns real?
Are leprechauns dangerous?
Do the Irish tend to wear really thick specs like I do?
Irish-looking facial hair
Hiding the fact that you really come from Swindon
What to do when actual Irish people start talking to you
Pretending that your middle name isn't Gerald

Disguising the fact that your father is the Fourteenth Earl
    of Wessex
Faking an Irish accent
Faking what the French might think is an Irish accent
Is my wife's name real?
Do the Irish usually write absolute filth to their spouses?
Is Donny Gall a place or a person?
Should I let people rub me for luck?
Places in Ireland that might be real
Ballydingus?
Castlegreyskull?
Killbillingham?
St Patrick's Day basics
Could the name Finnegan be possibly too Irish?
Making Guinness palatable
Lyrics to 'Danny Boy'
What is the most Irish-looking hat?

GANDHI

Hunger strike
Do hunger strikes have rules?
Do hunger strikes have invigilators?
How to cheat during hunger strikes
Rash decisions + reneging
Severe back-pedalling
Violent U-turning
Hamsters
Hamster cheeks
How do hamsters manage to cram all that extra food
     in their cheeks?
Concealing food
Concealing food around the human body
How many cashews can you conceal in an average
     armpit?
Hidden chunks of nougat + traditional robes
Broth + belly button
Foodstuffs that resemble loin cloth material
Man-sized cheese slices?
Edible eyewear made from liquorice?
Ham sandals?
Human hair + calories
Non-violent resistance + secret buffet
Pretending hunger strikes were all a great big joke
Other forms of protest
Protest + fun run?
Protest + bath full of baked beans?
Can you eat the beans when they're in the bath with you?
Cannibalism
Surreptitious cannibalism

Self-cannibalism
Which bits of the body grow back after nibbling?
What happens if I eat dandruff?
Am I going insane due to hunger?
Are there any sandwiches that are not considered food?
Fingernails + nutrition
Mashed potatoes + forgiveness
Some kind of samosa hat?
Pie-shaped furniture
Chicken and mushroom ottoman?
How to not think about scotch eggs
Hunting small insects
Trapping small insects
Eating small insects
Do my followers like being licked?

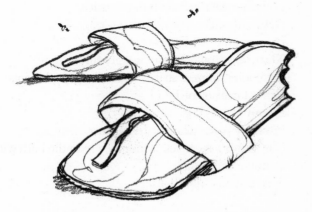

GEORGIA O'KEEFFE

Painting
Painting flowers
Painting flowers that really really look like vaginas
Issuing strenuous denials
Basing your whole career on painting flowers that really
    really look like vaginas
Firmly rejecting the notion that you paint flowers that
    really really look like vaginas
Continuing to paint flowers that really really look like
    vaginas
Threatening critics who claim you paint flowers that
    really really look like vaginas
Repeating your obviously gynaecological artistry
Angrily refuting claims
Rendering vaguely pornographic pot plants
Beginning litigation when such things are suggested
Horticultural crotch shots
Not touching that with a bargepole
Having exhibition after exhibition involving paintings
    that definitely look like fannies
Denying all knowledge of this phenomenon
Constant chuff-like daubs
Denying chuff-like daubs
A craggy gorge that's practically a cervix
Pretending to be blind
Leafy nether regions
Practising the phrase 'why, I've never heard of such
    a thing in my life'
Grassy knolls that wouldn't look out of place in
    an underpant

NO ACTUALLY, THAT ONE IS

Statements of heated disagreement

Vulvic representations in mixed media

Overt peevishness when this view is expressed

A well-drawn valley that is almost certainly a lady's undercarriage

Pretending you've never even picked up a paintbrush

Pube-like foliage in oils

Rebutting 'pube-like' interpretations

Being told by someone that they even recognize their own private area in a particular painting

Extensive rebuffing

How to react when someone shouts 'Wait a minute, that so-called jimson weed is a noo-noo'

Acting coy

Never looking at the garden centre in the same way again

Stringent dismissing

Fauna that absolutely looks like a labia

No

AGATHA CHRISTIE

Murders
Good murders
Dead good murders
Dead good juicy murders
Dead good juicy murders with actual juice
Stranglings
Plausible stranglings in large country houses
Non-ludicrous bludgeonings on fancy trains
Conceivable poisonings + Egyptian bodies of water
Beating an orphan to death with a swan + sympathetically
Involuntary spleen removal
Secret playground guillotine
UNEXPECTED PLOT TWISTS!
Believable garrotting on heathland
Random butler mutilation in the Home Counties

Pushing a sack of invalids into the path of a
    traction engine
Canine enslaughterment + by the docks
Reliable cleric exsanguination on a ferry
Stabbing a spinster a lot near Kent
Tainted meat expiration around the Gwent area
Groomsman + shotgun + arsehole + Lowestoft
ANOTHER UNEXPECTED PLOT TWIST!
Dropping a piano on a child
Dropping four pianos on a child
Acceptable heiress throat punchings around Mayfair
Pancreatic puncturing via St Pancras
Dispatching delightful old ladies with savage urine
    drownings
Turning nearby gadflies inside out
Shire horse + perineum tearing + viscount + Staines
Some kind of violent automatic eye popper in Hampshire
A THIRD STUPENDOUS PLOT TWIST!
Diplomat chainsaw sandwich
Pulling the guts out of a verger
Suffocating a really really nice person who doesn't
    deserve it
Bones snapping like cheap breadsticks + local swineherd
Hideous enforced dentistry on a road trip to Scarborough
A barrow boy getting a weasel shoved up his jap's eye
Atrocity + gentry + Cotswolds + umbrella stand
Just stabbing stabbing stabbing
WAYS TO MAKE IT ALL MAKE SENSE IN
    THE END!

ALBERT EINSTEIN

Regrets
Massive regrets
How to overcome massive regrets
How to overcome massive photographic regrets
Why did I let that guy take a picture of me with my
    tongue out?
Why does everyone only use that picture of me with my
    tongue out?
How to suppress embarrassing photographs
Suing photographers?
How to buy a negative
How to burn a negative
How many great scientists have had their picture taken
    with their tongue out?
Newton + tongue out?
Archimedes + tongue out?
Galileo + tongue out?
Should I try sticking my tongue out all the time to make
    it look normal?
Should I try rebranding myself as the 'tongue out'
    scientist?
How to stick your tongue out for long periods of time
Coping with a dry tongue
Can I use my physics knowledge to get out of any
    situation?
Physics + tongues
Physics + destroying photographs
Physics + destroying photographers
Arson?
Physical violence?

$$E = MC^2$$

E = ENERGY

M = PHOTOGRAPHS

C = THE DISTANCE MY
TONGUE IS STICKING OUT

Time travel?
How to build a time machine for the purposes of
    photographic destruction
Devising theories for time travel
Devising theories for time travel so you can destroy a
    photo where you have your tongue sticking out
What is time?
What is energy?
What is matter?
What's the matter?
Oh yeah, that photograph
$E = MC^2$ + revenge
Is it all relative?

HELEN KELLER

LKHIUGb;nlobobln'lk]p]pk phPIOHGBP
BSDHDL jhnwebpoj BDOIHPIWH
!!
XXVDIlmm
LDWOB0894y;m[
))*&(JK:L{OP
KWXOB
RoBBiee SAvaGGGGGGe
;JB98Y
Vf4prv[p
NLKPJK'P:N{JO}K{JB{JO|K{:NLHPI
ksdgfgsv
isdewpevjkpojvpr rlighp;n
)_+(*&*^vkj'
 hjlk;k 2§§§ po
OIUYT<MNBVLKJHGFPOIUG
#¢∞§¶•ªº¬∆˙∫^ƒ¥
    lklk lklk   lk;
GDGDDJ
HHHHHHHHHHHHHHHHHHHHHelen
><<><><>
:):(:):(:):(:):(
lXXXXXXXXX
f**ks**tc**ta**et**sb*m*o*e
POIUY)(*&98765BNM
What the hell is wrong with this computer?

PABLO PICASSO

Covering up the fact you can't draw hands + 'modern art'

ee cummings

letters
capital letters
who the hell do capital letters think they are
why are capital letters so uppity
why lowercase is the best case and uppercase is a
    rubbish case
generally obnoxious grammatical elements
full stops are getting mouthy now
why full stops are really dumb and ugly
are full stops and capital letters in cahoots
are full stops and capital letters out to get me
are full stops and capital letters in some sordid love tryst
why is everyone always telling me what to do +
    punctuation
no you've got an unorthodox orthography mr
    publisher man
the tyranny of colons
the bullying nature of ampersands
octothorp + bunch of dicks
checking under the bed every night for semi-colons
i bet its an asterisk making all those crank calls
how did that comma ruin my credit rating?
wait was that a question mark?
how did that question mark get in here?
oh my god there's more of them!
they've been joined by exclamation marks!
holy crap!?!
having a nice long lie down

AMELIA EARHART

Is the cockpit what I think it is?
How to stop flappers dancing on your wings
What exactly are goggles supposed to do?
Appropriate snacks for flight
Very small bag of peanuts?
Minuscule sachet of pretzels?
Pasta covered in goop covered in foil?
Would airplane food be good in my fledgling stand-up
    act?
Do we need some pointless heavily illustrated magazine
    selling useless crap for the flight?
Can I cram a really tiny toilet in the fuselage?
Do I just crap out the window + long distance flights
How much are ejector seats + chatty navigators
Is a joystick what I think it is?
Innovative promotional tie-in items
'Chicks with altitude' chemises
Saucy 'low flying' bloomers
Panty liners with wings
Is the undercarriage what I think it is?
Taking bets on how far you can fly
Sudden enormous gambling debts
Faking death + gambling debts + somewhere over
    the Atlantic
Good names to adopt + new life
'Amelia Noselung'?
'Amelia Lipspleen'?
'Amelia Chin-Stomachlining'?

JOHN LOGIE BAIRD

Good names for inventions
Stare Box?
Gaze Cube?
Watch Hole?
Tiny Theatre In Your House That's Not Really There?
Picture Prison?
Eye Cage?
Non-Fished Aquarium (With Images)?
Johnnies Jolly Jukebox?
Painting Gone Movey-Weird?
Looky Loo?
The Magical Bread Box?
Tube O'Boobs?
Gallery of Dreck?
Corner Warmer?
Loud Mad Furniture?
Cinema But Fairly Worse?
Grim Optinaut?
The Glass Mastubatium?
The Cheapest Lil Babysitter in the West?
View Lump?
Timed Screened Disappointments?
The Cabinet of Angry Tuneless Dreams?
Convenient Hate Spewer?
Logie's Spastic Trauma?
Grandma Distractor?
The Life Ruiner?
Sick Window?
Haircuts on Parade?
Wooden Pondering Well?

Brain Deflater?
Pointlessness Squared?
Where to Point the Sofa?
The Argue-Box 2000?
Baird's Splendorarium?
Time Evaporator?
Marriage Saver?
Only Friend Be-er?
Thing That Sells Cereal from Far Away?

COCO CHANEL

Big blue smock?
Small blue smock?
Smaller blue smock?
Tiny blue smock?
Small blue blouse?
Small taupe blouse?
Big taupe blouse?
Medium-sized taupe blouse?
Enormous orange bodice?

CHANEL TUNNEL

Tiny yellow dungarees?
Average length charcoal jodhpurs?
Unrealistically minuscule tangerine chemise?
Well-proportioned mustard cardigan?
Completely overrated mustard cardigan?
Overtly French pebbledashed tunic?
One piece biscuit bathing suit?
Moderate ball gown that's just painted on?
Succulent rose hued anklets?
Edible purple boob tube?
Medium-sized horse-coloured pantomime horse costume?
Titchy mauve headdress?
Flamboyantly beige activity jerkin?
Unprepossessing sandy hand bangle?
Portly rhubarb fishnets?
Dangerously well-defined alabaster slingbacks?
Sarcastic fluorescent flip-flops?
Pointlessly textured sick-coloured dress?
Unenthusiastically textured sick-coloured dress?
Untextured sick-coloured dress?
Sick-coloured dress that's the size of an aircraft hanger?
Creamy dress that's the size of an aircraft hanger?
Non-creamy dress that's the size of an aircraft hanger?
Non-creamy dress that's not the size of an aircraft hanger?
Normal-sized dress that's not creamed?
Little dress that's not creamed?
Little non-creamed dress?
Little black windbreaker?
Little black trestle table?
Little black dressing gown?
COME ON COCO YOU'VE NEARLY GOT THIS!

WINSTON CHURCHILL

How to conduct a war while very drunk
What's that Hitler up to now?
Could Nazi be an acronym for something?
'Nasty angry zealoty idiots' + but in German
What exactly is a hun?
Is hun short for a hundred?
Are huns tasty?
Why you should never go to war on an empty stomach
Entire sheep's flank + breakfast?
How much venison is too much venison?
Literal goldfish bowls full of brandy
Ever-so-slightly larger cigars
Could I fit in a meal between dinner and supper?
Dupper?
Eveningsies?
Dinner Two: Supperish?
Getting the doorways of the Cabinet war rooms lightly
    greased
Map of all the water closets closest to me at any given time
Blaming noxious gravy farts on nearby generals
Effective jowl management
Bow-ties that make my neck look more normal
Why does this stupid war keep interrupting my eating?
Speeches
Making speeches
Should I get those elocution lessons?
Should I provide some sort of bib for people when I'm
    making speeches?
Disguising speech impediments with positive hand
    gestures

How many fingers am I holding up?

When I hold up two fingers why don't people realize
    I'm telling them how many heart attacks I'm
    currently having?

Where do people like to fight?

Pub car park?

Night omnibus?

Wedding reception?

Is Vera Lynn single?

Is Vera Lynn good to go?

Vera Lynn + nudie pics

Would flying in a spitfire impress Vera Lynn?

Could I fit in a spitfire?

Good names for battles

'Battle of Blighty'?

'Battle of This Country I'm
    Currently In'?

'Battle of Not Germany'?

Is the Battle Of The Bulge
    about me?

WRONG

RIGHT

173

ADOLF HITLER

Balls

Balls + number

How many balls are normal?

How many testicles should a human man have?

Scrotal basics + Austrian

Can you turn one big one into two smaller ones?

How do girls feel about freakish gonads?

Turning irregular nut numbers to your advantage

Testicular examination + time saving

Harder to be hit in the groin

Roomier scrotum

Faking bollock deficiencies through ballsack shading

When is the best time to mention the testicle thing on
    a date?

Testicular information + leaks

Testicular information + not those sort of leaks, the
    information kind

Dirt on Churchill + catchy songs

Where is my other love egg?

Führer's love egg + Poland?

Good excuses to invade Poland and search for a
    missing knacker

Is my number of sex orbs affecting my decision making?

Getting those special trousers made

Did I hear giggling + Reichstag

Would a peculiar moustache distract from my nutbag
    deficiencies?

Good names for lone testes

'Tony Aloney'?

'Pistachi-No Nut'?

'Very private part'?
Cobbler transplants
Undescending undescended plums
Possible location of missing testicles in London
    music venue
Invasion plans + glandular location
Protecting remaining testicles
Some kind of armoured truss?
Electrified thong?
Ways to secrete mousetraps in your underpants
Coming to terms with your lack of conkers
Support groups + Berlin area
How many testicles does Stalin have?

ENID BLYTON

Suitable subjects for children's literature

Ponies?

Trains?

A strange hybrid elf-gnome creature?

What if the strange hybrid elf-gnome creature had a
    supporting cast of weirdos?

What actually is Noddy?

Is it weird that I find Noddy so completely disturbing?

Ensuring children are terrified of Noddy forever

Just how racist should my children's stories be?

What's a reasonable amount of books to write before lunch?

Good numbers for famous child gangs

Famous four?

Famous six?

Famous 90?

Famous 4.2?

Ways to shoehorn a secret passage into every story

Are all foreigners evil?

Smugglers

Blaming things on smugglers

Blaming everything on smugglers

Ensuring children are terrified of smugglers forever

Best time of night for slap-up feasts

Can you slap-up any other meals?

Is ginger beer the only drink you have lashings of?

Good names for child lesbians

Boarding schools

Writing stories about boarding schools

Keeping your job with the boarding-school marketing
    board a secret

How to make talking trees less unnerving
Ensuring children are terrified of talking trees forever
How many children do I add to a gang before its secret?
Secret pi?
Secret half dozen?
Secret absolute zero?
What's my thing for numbered children?
Can the addition of numbered children improve
    any story?
Cannibal psychiatrist plays mind games with an FBI
    agent + numbered children
Suave superspy outwits evil criminal mastermind
    + numbered children
Carpenters son unexpectedly becomes the messiah
    + numbered children
Why do people say I keep writing the same thing?
Why do people say I keep writing the same thing?

ERNEST HEMINGWAY

Synonyms for courage
Synonyms for fighting
Synonyms for drinking
Synonyms for skirmish
Synonyms for battle
Synonyms for bloodshed
Convincing virginity loss stories
Synonyms for adventure
Synonyms for hunting
Synonyms for grappling
Synonyms for fury
Synonyms for bravery
Synonyms for honour
Things virgins don't say
Synonyms for bullfighter
Synonyms for fisherman
Synonyms for soldier
Synonyms for explorer
Synonyms for spy
Synonyms for boxer
Living a lie
Synonyms for bruising
Synonyms for rupture
Synonyms for suture
Synonyms for blood
Synonyms for wound
Synonyms for stabbing
Advantages of extensive virginity
Synonyms for warfare
Synonyms for safari

Synonyms for matador
Synonyms for firearms
Synonyms for brutality
Synonyms for boat
How to talk to girls
Synonyms for strength
Synonyms for vigour
Synonyms for power
Synonyms for might
Synonyms for machismo
Synonyms for he-man
Losing virginity + solo

SAMUEL BECKETT

Roughly how many words should be in a play?
Lowest possible number of words in a play
Lowest possible number of words in a play + legally
Do they pay you per word or for how long the play lasts?
Are pauses a good way to pad theatrical events out?
How long should a pause be?
Longest pauses ever + breaking world records
Do they still pay you if the characters aren't saying
    anything?
Good ideas for plays
A king of lions?
Crazy opera ghost?
Violin player + roof?
Story about people near the west side of somewhere?
Mounds?
Plays featuring mounds
Can I corner the theatrical mound market?
Big mounds
Big dirty mounds
Big dirty mounds + Billie Whitelaw
Basic mound choreography
French for 'mound'
'Le mound'?
Big words
Big words in plays
Are really long words better than really long pauses?
Saying really long words really slowly
What is the longest quietest word?
Bowler hats
Bowler hats in plays

Can I corner the theatrical bowler hat market?
Bowler hat rental
Cheap bowler hat rental
How to make your own convincing-looking bowler hat
Could I have a play with a mound wearing a bowler hat?
Nobel Prize
Nobel Prize + front runners
Nobel Prize + judges
Nobel Prize + judges + bribery
Swedish for 'bribe'
'Brïbe'?
Should I just have Godot turn up and save everybody
    some time?

JACKSON POLLOCK

Caricatures
Setting yourself up as a caricaturist
How much do caricaturists make?
How to draw caricatures
How to draw noses
Why can't I draw noses?
Should I give up my dream of being a boardwalk
    caricaturist?
Paint huffing
Overcoming disappointment + paint huffing
Is my paint huffing problem out of control?
Huffing paint and then throwing the paint all over the
    place in anger
Cleaning up spilt paint

Wait + spilt paint + cha-ching?
Would anyone buy these spilt-paint things?
Am I just phoning it in?
Should I learn to paint actual things?
Should I paint ponies?
Do ponies have noses?
Should I huff some more paint and then see what happens?
Interns
Interns + painting
Interns + painting + just throwing it all over the place
Am I a genius?
Or am I just messy?
Am I a fraud?
Am I a bit of a fraud but my heart is in the right place?
What's better: really really small paintings or really really
    big paintings?
Why did my cleaner quit?
How long should I pretend my paintings take me to finish?
Why do I never hear from the paintings-by-numbers people?
Why do I never hear from those magic-eye-paintings people?
Moving
Moving apartments + getting deposit back
Landlord + no deposit + 'excessive' paint removal
Definition of excessive
Disputes with landlords
Small claims court + landlords
Exciting names for paintings
'My old landlord is a dick'?
'Old Drippy'?
'Splatarama'?
'Check Out the Streaks On That One'?
Why noses in art are over-rated

MARILYN MONROE

How to meet + horndog presidents
How to meet + horndog presidents' brothers
How to meet + horndog presidents' wives
How to meet + grumpy baseball stars
How to meet + leftie playwrights in glasses
How to meet + hefty playwrights in saunas
How to meet + frizzy-haired scientists
How to meet + high-level mafiosos
How to meet + short stocky mafiosos
How to meet + blue-eyed crooners
How to meet + blue-eyed crooners with mafioso
    connections
How to meet + intense method actors who will probably
    get really fat
How to meet + insane millionaires with big planes and
    long fingernails
How to meet + prosperous influential movie producers
How to meet + people who pretend to be prosperous
    influential movie producers even though they're
    wearing a barrel instead of clothes
How to meet + key grips who can keep their mouth shut
How to meet + best boys who live up to the title
How to meet + gaffers who are not into bondage
How to meet + silent-film stars who carried a cane
How to meet + non-silent-film stars who carried a Kane
How to meet + cowboys
How to meet + cowgirls
How to meet + cowpokes
How to meet + old timey prospectors who say 'Gold!
    Gold!' and do a jig in celebration

HAPPY BIRTHDAY TO
[INSERT PRESIDENT'S NAME]

How to meet + actors with thin pencil moustaches
How to meet + actors with ludicrously bushy moustaches
    and massive sideburns to match
How to meet + men beneath air-propelling sidewalk grills
How to meet + men in drag in jazz bands
How to meet + men who express a hair colour preference
How to meet + any popes on the turn
How to meet + Middle-Eastern sultans
How to meet + middle-ranking mailmans
How to meet + that guy that cleans my drapes
How to meet + that guy that fixed my guttering
How to meet + that guy that delivered my hoagie
How to meet + that guy over there, the one with the limp
How to meet + anyone who actually turns out to not be a
    total asshole

NEIL ARMSTRONG

Space
What is space?
Things that happen in space
Things that happen in space + male genitals
Pressure
Space pressure
Space pressure + male genitals
Zero-gravity gonad explosions
Will my scrotum blow up like a space hopper in space?
Does the name space hopper come from space?
Chances of penile enrupturement during blast off
How much g-force can my knackers take?
Getting Buzz to stop scaring you about potential space
    cobbler damage
Hiding places
Good hiding places for an astronaut
Excellent hiding places in the Cape Canaveral area
What if the moon men are really into human balls?
Puking in your space hat
Soiling a moon buggy
Crying in a command module
Astro germs?
Space lizards?
Moon crabs?
Are giant moon crabs real?
Giant moon crabs + astronaut genitals
Getting Buzz to stop talking about giant moon crabs and
    my genitals
What if I catch my scrotum on a crater?
Disguises

Plausible disguises
Plausible disguises for an astronaut on the run
Can I balance a cowboy hat on top of my spaceman hat?
Can't we just fake the whole moon-landing thing?
Stanley Kubrick's phone number
Running away and starting new life
Running away and starting new life + astronaut
Pseudonyms
Real sounding pseudonyms
'Rodrigo Sanchez'?
'Rodrigo Sanchez' + astronaut
How do I poop without gravity?
Taking one giant leap quickly in the opposite direction

JIM MORRISON

Naming a band after whatever is directly in front of
    you right now
'The Pants'?
'The Lamps'?
'The Groovy Windowsills'?
Native American spirit guides
Good Native American spirit guides
Native American spirit guides who won't dick you around
    and make you walk into walls
Why is my Native American spirit guide so mean to me?
Songs about firelighters
Managing very curly hair
Plus-sized leather pants
How to write pretentious lyrics
How to write really really pretentious lyrics
How to avoid accusations of pretension by insisting
    you're a poet
Things to do during guitar solos
Basic recipes for one + guitar solos
Teach yourself juggling + guitar solos
Innovative yoyo manoeuvres + guitar solos
Does taking too much acid really affect your chutney
    I mean brain?
Do Jefferson Airplane have any openings?
Obscene stagecraft for beginners
Regal reptile positions
President + crocodile?
Prime Minister + turtle?
Benign dictator + terrapin?
Do lizards need kings?

Legitimate non-mammalian monarchy structures
Am I like Aquaman but for lizards?
Attempting to summon thousands of lizards to do your
    bidding
Mass lizard dispersal
How to be in a band with someone called Ray
Ideal weather conditions for riders
Inventive ways to describe strange people
Cities where women usually come from
Good titles for solo albums
'Desert Gecko Sun Highway Cherokee Highway
    LA Lady'?
'Why Guitar Solos Are Overrated'?
'Jim Morrisongs!'?
Best places to take heroin in French bathrooms
Sad ways to die young
Easy ways to clutter up French cemeteries

SATAN

Angel + promotion opportunities
Dealing with an over-demanding boss
Do I have a case for unfair dismissal?
Why are seraphim such pricks?
Falls + workplace compensation
Why does absolutely everything clash with red?
Why is it always so bloody hot in here?
How long do I have to wait for this place to freeze over?
What are my horns for?
Coping with overcrowding
Coping with paperwork + taking on many forms
What am I supposed to do with all these idle hands?
Realizing that idle hands are the worst hands to do
    anything with
Idle hands + employment tribunal
Getting the smell of goat out of curtains
Necronomicon for dummies
Getting goths to back off
Will I ever grow to love heavy metal?
Re-gifting Ouija boards
Good ideas for infinite torment
Some kind of butt hammer?
A scrotal pulley system?
Really bad paper cuts?
Do the damned have bodies?
How are the damned even feeling any of this?
Surely this is all a waste of time
Keeping millions of naughty cavemen entertained
Cleaning tips + circles of hell
Dante + needlessly complicated

Paradise Lost + libel?
Why do I find goats so creepy?
How do I get all of these bats out of here?
Shaking off my 'bad guy' image
Should I get new representation?
Increasing sympathy for me
Fending off the romantic advances of witches
Fending off the romantic advances of bishops
Fending off the romantic advances of fiddle players
Pay scales + imps v demons?
Blaming the smell of sulphur on others
Literally everyone cool ever is here
Who is up there?
Why is the phone signal so crappy down here?
Souls + resale value
Why don't I ever appear in food?
Terror + everlasting + darkest dreams of man + pot pourri
How come the only animal I get is the goat?
Why pitchforks + obvious lack of hay
How not to look smug when winning